THE
JUDICIOUS MARRIAGE OF MR HOOKER
AND THE BIRTH OF
THE LAWS OF ECCLESIASTICAL POLITY

The
Judicious Marriage of Mr Hooker
and the Birth of
The Laws of Ecclesiastical Polity

BY

C. J. SISSON

Lord Northcliffe Professor
of Modern English Literature in the
University of London

OCTAGON BOOKS

A DIVISION OF FARRAR, STRAUS AND GIROUX

New York   1974

First published 1940

Reprinted 1940
by permission of Cambridge University Press

OCTAGON BOOKS
A DIVISION OF FARRAR, STRAUS & GIROUX, INC.
19 Union Square West
New York, N. Y. 10003

Library of Congress Cataloging in Publication Data

Sisson, Charles Jasper, 1885-1966.
The judicious marriage of Mr. Hooker and the birth of The laws of ecclesiastical polity.

Reprint of the 1940 ed. published at the University Press, Cambridge, Eng.

1. Hooker, Richard, 1553 or 4-1600. Ecclesiastical polity.   I. Title.

BV649.H9S5   1974   262   74-9652
ISBN 0-374-97465-9

Printed in U.S.A. by
NOBLE OFFSET PRINTERS, INC.
NEW YORK, N.Y. 10003

To

V. K. S.

pariter felix ac R. H.

C. J. S.

CONTENTS

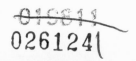

Appendices page

Pedigrees

Index

PREFACE

Richard Hooker loved the truth, and pursued it. His memory deserves no less. This book is an attempt to furnish the truth upon some matters of importance to him. In the long and crowded roll of great English men of letters there is no figure of greater significance to the instructed mind than Hooker. The beauty of his life and character inspired a masterpiece of English biography in Izaak Walton's narrative. His own life's work is a monument of pure and splendid prose style and of lucid philosophic thought, based on unsurpassed scholarship in the vast field of his theme. The book itself is a milestone in the history of a great English institution and of religious thought. Both the man and his book are therefore of the highest interest. The story of the actual writing and publication of the book has an exceptional significance, in relation both to Hooker's life and to the history of his time. Biography and bibliography of necessity go hand in hand in search of the full truth. New documentary information has led me to a narrative and an interpretation which are radically at variance with accepted views of both biographical and bibliographical history, and has furnished a mass of intimate detail of great interest.

On the biographical side, the authority of Walton's *Life* cannot lightly be assailed. It would be difficult to find a witness of greater credibility than Izaak Walton. A man of unblemished character, of a sweet nature, and of high repute in his own day, his qualities are reflected in his writings. His testimony therefore carries with it all the weight of his unassailable candour. Walton's *Lives* invite assent and acceptance by their literary quality, by their sympathetic disinterestedness, and also by the evident pains taken by their author to explore and exhaust all available sources of informa-

tion. Walton's veracity cannot be impugned. But the
information furnished to him bears no such certificate of
disinterestedness. Contemporary evidence from informal
personal sources, though precious and irreplaceable, must
always be subject to suspicion, and its authority is to be
measured by the quality of the witness. In the light of new
facts, Walton's *Life of Hooker* is found to be a striking
example of the distortions of truth seen through the prism
of personal recollections and traditional story, with no clear
distinction possible between deliberate ill-will and the too-
ready acceptance of not ungrateful scandal, on the part of
Walton's informants.

Nothing, for example, could appear to be better authenticated than Walton's account of Hooker's marriage. We
find two independent sources of authority converging in his
pages. He had his own direct information from his Cranmer
relations, who were intimately connected with Hooker as
with Walton. He further had corroboration from Fuller's
Worthies. Fuller wrote in his *Church History* that Hooker
lived and died a bachelor, but corrected himself in his
Worthies, stating then that

he had Wife and Children, though indeed such as were neither
to his comfort, when living, nor credit when Dead.

The manner of his correction indicates the discovery of new
information, and its claim to authenticity is greatly increased
by Fuller's marginal note giving his authority. This he had,
he writes, from an unimpeachable source,

from the mouth of his sister, lately living at Hogsden, near
London.

Yet the full story of Hooker's domestic life, closely related
as it was to his public life, together with certain unhappy
sequels in Chancery to his death, gives a reasonable explanation of this concurrence of family traditions, while at the
same time invalidating them.

A still odder story is that of the attack upon Hooker's memory, told by Walton with great reticence. In Bishop Gauden's *Life* it takes a different form, and is related in great detail, as in Prince's *Worthies of Devon*. Gauden tells how Hooker was waylaid by an unscrupulous woman and her bully, and how to avoid scandal Hooker parted with his purse and was subsequently preyed upon by them at his lodgings, for months together, to his great distress of mind and estate; how his friend Sandys saw his tormentors at his lodging and made enquiry, how Hooker pretended he was merely giving charity to the poor, but at last told the truth, and how Sandys rescued him and sent the blackmailers to Bridewell. A more improbable story would be difficult to invent, and indeed it involves impossibilities. One wonders at how many removes from the original facts this tradition reached Gauden and Walton, despite Gauden's assertion of his immediate authority.

The supersession of Gauden's *Life* by Walton's also arouses curiosity. Walton's *Life*, we know, was commissioned by Gilbert Sheldon, Archbishop of Canterbury, soon after the appearance of Gauden's *Life*. Was Sheldon dissatisfied with Gauden's *Life*, either because of its historical inadequacy or its literary defects? Certainly Gauden did little else than repeat old errors, such as Fuller's early statement about Hooker's lifelong bachelorhood, or propagate new errors. And his manner of writing is intolerably stilted and vulgar. But it may be that high policy was involved. Was it necessary to discredit both Gauden's account of Hooker and his edition of the *Ecclesiastical Polity* (including for the first time Book Seven) to which it was prefaced? Gauden was looked upon with great suspicion by the High Church, and his record was against him in many ways. The Seventh Book was by no means entirely palatable in the form in which it appeared. Is it possible, then, that Hooker and the manuscripts of the last three Books of his treatise, left behind him at his death, became pawns in the strategy of the Church of England

under Charles II as the first four Books were under Elizabeth?
It is an unhappy thought, but it is not to be rejected. The
whole trend of Walton's *Life*, while preserving intact the
honour and the sanctity of Hooker, the hero of the earlier
wars of the Church, throws suspicion upon the fate of his
manuscripts, the story being supported and made more
credible by the repeated attacks upon Hooker's wife, who is
held responsible for the vandalism which, we are told, ruined
his literary legacy to the Church. It may well be that Walton's
brief was carefully prepared for him. Certainly circumstantial stories came to him, and were inserted by him, which
are demonstrably impossible and false. There is, for example,
the story of Mrs Hooker's summoning to London, her confession, and death in 1600.

If so, the choice was well made. Walton was, after all,
an old man of seventy when the task was laid upon him.
He was a most faithful son of the Church. And no other
writer could be trusted to give such personal authority to a
biography, to give such currency to its contents by virtue
of his invincible liveliness, humour and zestfulness, to make
a masterpiece of a piece of propaganda. It was an unscrupulous age, and an age when men's thoughts were much
affected by literary skill properly used and directed, even
when, as surely in this instance, unconscious of its aim.

It would be hazardous to go further than to record a
distinct uneasiness in one's mind in these considerations. But
there is no doubt that the authority of Walton's *Life*, as a
record of facts, may now be taken to be gravely undermined
in respect of many of its most picturesque incidents. The new
information to be set forth with all its implications, in the
following pages, is derived from the unimpeachable documents of a Court of Law,[1] and from the evidence of living
witnesses who were Hooker's contemporaries. And it is

---

[1] Unimpeachable, that is to say, as documents. I am aware, none
better, of the need for reserve in approaching statements made in such
documents.

irreconcilable with much of the traditional information upon which Walton founded his *Life of Hooker*.

As for the history of the actual writing and publishing of Hooker's great book, little information has hitherto been on record, and that little appears to be erroneous. Walton tells us of the writing of *The Laws of Ecclesiastical Polity* during Hooker's retreat in the quiet solitude of his rectory at Boscombe, free from the distractions of his life in London. It seems clear that he never in fact went to Boscombe, and that residence in London and consultation there with others interested in his project were essential to the planning and the writing of the book. The greater part of it was written, appropriately enough, under the very shadow of St Paul's, where he had first made himself known to London, in his sermon of 1581, as a possible champion of the Church. Among his circle of friends and advisers he found a wife and a home and happiness in his father-in-law's house. There was his study, and the focus and meeting-place of his consultants. And Churchman's servant, a skilled and careful penman, served Hooker as his secretary and amanuensis, who made fair copies of his draft manuscript for the press.

When an important section of the book was thus made ready for printing, no publisher could be found for it. It only achieved publication by the financial backing of those who saw its importance, or even planned it, as part of the strategy of the political campaign in which they were engaged. Hooker's *Ecclesiastical Polity* is probably the greatest book ever published, and published of necessity, on commission.

The details of the transaction, covering most aspects of book-production, and checked as they may be by the close study of the early editions of Hooker's book, are of high bibliographical interest. It was this aspect of the material that justified its presentation in the University of Cambridge as the Sandars Lectures in Bibliography in 1938. But it is of great biographical interest too. For we have a picture of Hooker being pressed to hasten on his work to meet political exigencies, of his grief and perturbation at the prospect of his labour being wasted, of his anxiety that his work when printed should be accessible to thin purses, and of the great day when at last it was in print, when he received the copies promised to him and sat down to parcel up one of the first with a letter to the great Burleigh, hoping to convince him and to enlist him among the true supporters of the cause he had so profoundly at heart.

The publication of the first four Books of the *Ecclesiastical Polity* in its *editio princeps* may now be confidently dated 1593, instead of Walton's 1594. And the date is significant. It was essential, for political reasons, that it should appear in time to support the moves which led to a Conventicle Act, presented simultaneously in Parliament.

Finally, Walton's account of the fate of the manuscripts left by Hooker at his death, both of the unfinished Books VI–VIII of the *Ecclesiastical Polity* and of minor works, must be subjected to the correction of facts derived from first-hand evidence in detail. The story now to be told exonerates Mrs Hooker. It indicates a great and lively interest on the part of Hooker's coadjutors which presently faded, with the passage of time, and with lukewarmness due to the emergence of doctrinal differences. It also relates a strange negligence in the final disposal of these manuscripts, which lay forgotten for years, their chief trustee having turned his attention to his other concerns. Had not Corpus Christi, his own College, remembered him when others forgot, Hooker's minor writings might never have been published and might have vanished.

I owe my thanks to the University of Cambridge which, when it elected me to read the Sandars Lectures, obliged me to complete work upon material with which I had procrastinated, and conferred honour beyond desert. I had helpful suggestions upon some problems of detail from Mgr Philip Hallett, Canon Shirley, Headmaster of the King's School, Canterbury, Mr John Butt, Miss Jeffries Davis, and

Mr R. T. D. Sayle, Master of the Merchant Taylors' Company. To him, and to Mr Tewson, Accountant of the Company, I am also indebted for putting their beautifully kept records at my disposal. Pepys' copy of the *Ecclesiastical Polity* was brought to my notice by Mr Turner, Fellow of Magdalene College, Cambridge, and Pepys Librarian. My colleague Mr Geoffrey Tillotson engaged himself upon a thoroughgoing analysis of the early editions of Hooker, and allowed me to check my own findings from his more complete study. A complete Bibliography of Hooker would be a most welcome contribution from his pen. The Rector of St Augustine's, Watling Street, Dr Ross, most kindly placed at my disposal the Registers of his parish, which I found to be so rich in facts concerning the family life of Hooker and his intimates, as did the Vicar of Enfield, the Rev. G. W. Daisley. The Sequestrators of St John's, Chipstead, where Hooker's daughters lived with their guardian John Huntley, and where one of them lies buried, permitted me to examine their Registers, at inconvenience to themselves. My colleague Miss Winifred Husbands kindly contributed the Index, thus ensuring that one part of the book would be beyond reproach, and also read the proofs with vigilant skill. In the preface to a book much concerned with printers and printing, and that *non sine pulvere*, it would be unpardonable to omit a tribute to the spirit and the craftsmanship of the University Press of Cambridge, whose predecessors in Hooker's own day were enlisted in the opposition to the cause for which he stood. To the preserving spirit of the English people, to the long generations of the keepers of English records, and to the present custodians of this treasure and their courteous helpfulness, this study owes everything else.

The outbreak of war has prevented me from making certain further investigations which I had in mind, e.g. in the Merchant Taylors' records. Enforced absence from London has been an impediment in the final stages of the book. Fortunately I was provided with photostats of the principal documents, and I may trust that no serious error has escaped correction, except any due to my own faulty judgment. For any such errors, and for my conclusions in general, I must be held solely responsible.

C. J. SISSON

UNIVERSITY COLLEGE, LONDON
AT ABERYSTWYTH
March 1940

Chapter I

THE JUDICIOUS MARRIAGE OF
MR HOOKER

§i. THE IMPORTANCE OF HOOKER'S
MARRIAGE

A great man's life-work is not always happily linked up
with the circumstances of his ordinary human relations.
Posterity is apt to think ill of the wife of a genius. It has
always been assumed that Ann Hathaway counted for nothing
in Shakespeare's poetry and drama, and for little in his life.
Shakespeare, we are instructed, achieved fame and fulfilled
his destiny by escaping to London from Ann and from the
crippling chains of an ill-judged marriage. 'Good men have
often ill wives', wrote Robert Burton, a bachelor himself.
Ben Jonson married a shrew, as Drummond reported from
Ben's own mouth. Much has been written about the un-
suitability of Anne Powell for the position of wife to Milton.
Molière's wife, it seems, helped considerably to embitter his
life. Xantippe and Dame Alice clogged the heels of Socrates
and More. One might lengthen the list. So Richard Hooker,
we have believed for three hundred years on the authority
of Walton's *Life*, groaned beneath the burden of a worthless
and dowerless wife, trapped into marriage with her, yet
staggered on despite his heavy cross to achieve one of the
monuments of English thought and literature, his treatise on
The Laws of Ecclesiastical Polity.

It is a depressing picture, and it offends against one's sense
of the fitness of things. It is a theme fit for satire, feeding
such cynicism as is wholly alien to Hooker's great mind and
kindly spirit. Hooker deserved a true helpmate, as Walton

observed. It is with the greater joy, therefore, that a new story may now be told, this time a true story, which satisfies our taste as well as our understanding. For it would seem that in no matter was 'the judicious Mr Hooker' more judicious than in his marriage, or at any rate more fortunate. The circumstances which led to his marriage determined also, and made possible, the writing of his great book, which was indeed the immortal child of that marriage. The book has survived, indestructible as all the products of a high human spirit, for centuries after the death of the four daughters who were the mortal fruits of the union of Richard Hooker with Joan Churchman, their names the sweet symphony of Alice, Cicely, Jane and Margaret. Even before Izaak Walton came to immortalize the image of the man Hooker, the very memory of the two sons who also blessed that marriage had perished.

Hooker's marriage, and his relations with John Churchman and his family, are now to appear as an essential part of the setting for his life's work. But these human relations are closely bound up with those factors in religious and political history which called forth his treatise on Church government, and which hitherto have been considered in isolation from his private life. They are of the utmost importance for the understanding of Hooker's work, and they call for our attention first, in this story of the birth of a great book and of the life of its author.

§ ii. THE THEME OF
THE LAWS OF ECCLESIASTICAL POLITY

'Hooker would not have been', wrote Cardinal Newman, 'but for the existence of Catholics and Puritans, the defeat of the former and the rise of the latter.' It should be added that of these two conditions which determined the writing of *The Laws of Ecclesiastical Polity*, the rise of the Puritans was that which was decisive. The challenge of the Catholics was already receding into the background when Hooker began meditating his great work. Its long Preface is directed to the address of those who put their hopes in Geneva and borrowed their convictions concerning Church government from that home of doctrinaire theorists. And the real danger to the Church of England, now triumphant, blew in gusts from those Alpine winds.

If the English bishops were to be deposed, they would fall, not before rival bishops, but before elders and presbyters. The Church itself was riddled with doubters and with open zealots. Archbishop Whitgift complained to Burleigh concerning the very Bishops: far from suppressing nonconformist ministers, he wrote, 'they offend rather, the most of them, on the contrarie part'. The Universities taught Calvinistic and Presbyterian views in public lectures, and at Oxford Hooker himself came under the influence of Dr Reynoldes, subsequently Head of his College, who led the Puritan wing of the Church there. The Inns of Court were no safe abode for the good churchman. When Hooker was elected Master of the Temple in 1585 he was involved at once in hot controversy with the famous Walter Travers, the lecturer or preacher there, whose afternoon sermons invoked Geneva to exorcise Hooker's morning Canterbury. Little models of the Genevan pattern were erected here and there in England, and the unofficial salvation of our country was set on foot, undermining the scheme for official means of grace. A flood of surreptitious literature poured into England from abroad, furnishing further argumentative ammunition to reinforce convictions already strong with fanatic zeal. The vivacious Marprelate controversy ran its mad course, in which the Church had little but ineffective heavy guns to reply to the more exciting rockets and crackers of the unbridled Puritans. The crisis, both political and intellectual, was urgent. The imminent danger from abroad, it is true, had receded in 1588 when the devastated Spanish Armada limped home again. But the guerilla war within our frontiers was growing in audacity. The Queen's Council was determined to use sharper weapons against internal disruption. And the need for better intellectual artillery became more evident against opponents of undoubted mettle.

A certain Dr John Bridges had launched a battleship of a book in 1587, some fourteen hundred pages of it, to defend the position of the Church. The Marprelatists made high holiday with this *Defence of the Government established in the Church of England for Ecclesiastical Matters*, and it sank both by its own weight and under its added tophamper of ridicule. The book, indeed, recalls the unkind comment of Jenkyns, Master of Balliol, to the Tractarian Ward in 1844, upon his *Ideal of a Christian Church.* 'Well, Ward, your book is like yourself, fat, awkward and ungainly.' Bridges' treatise, wrote a Marprelatist, was 'very briefly comprehended in a portable book, if your horse be not too weake, of an hundred threescore and twelve sheets of good Demie paper'. John Windet, cousin of Richard Hooker, was the printer, and the experience seems to have daunted his courage, as similar ventures disillusioned other London printers of bulky controversial orthodoxy for which there was no market.

The time was ripe, it was thought, for a treatment of the problem of nonconformity which should rise above mere controversy and be proof against guerilla warfare. Richard Hooker was the right man. His character and his learning were known to Oxford. Edwin Sandys, successively Bishop of Worcester, Bishop of London, and Archbishop of York, was his benevolent patron, and Sir Edwin, his son, was Hooker's intimate friend and a leading spirit in the conflict. Hooker dedicated himself to his task, and his life was so ordered, as we shall see, that he could give himself up to his studies, and consult at his ease with friends and advisers in London. The projected book was to carry with it the full authority, not only of the undisputed learning and persuasive humanity of its author, but also that of the deputed spokesman of the Church, advised and aided by lay notables, and countenanced by the spiritual heads of the Church, Archbishops Sandys of York and Whitgift of Canterbury.

Hooker's appointment to the Mastership of the Temple, indeed, was an announcement that battle was about to be joined. Walter Travers and his kinsman by marriage Richard Hooker now stood forth in the lists, the Hector and the Achilles of the War of the Churches. Travers had shown his prowess in the field with his Latin treatise *Ecclesiasticae Disciplinae*, a work of much learning. Cartwright himself, the general of the Puritan host, had translated the work into English. Archbishop Whitgift realized more fully than ever, when this book came out from a Cambridge press in 1584, a reprint of the Geneva edition of 1580, the inconvenience of allowing printing at Cambridge, the spiritual home of the nonconformist movement, where the same strict censorship could not be maintained as at London. It was in all probability printed by Thomas Thomas. Whitgift wrote to Burleigh on 30 June 1584, indicating his uneasiness, adding that the book in question was 'veri factius and full of untruthes'. 'Ever sens I hard that they had a printer in Chambridg I dyd greatlie feare that this and such like inconveniences wold follow', he observed. It would be convenient that the book should be burned, he concluded. But it was far from easy to move Burleigh in the matter. Burleigh was, indeed, an obstacle to be overcome by the Church in its efforts to establish its discipline. Travers was, after all, chosen by him to be tutor to his own son.

A champion was needed to meet Travers on his own ground and on equal terms. Travers had much support. Cambridge again sent out an assault in print, when *The Harmony of the Church*, so strangely confused with Drayton's harmless collection of hymns, appeared in 1586. This time Whitgift communicated with the Vice-Chancellor of the University to assist in the suppression of the book, which had been refused a licence in London. By this time Hooker was already deep in the preparation of his counter-attack. And in the meantime the two champions used the Temple Church as a tilting-ground. Their alarums and excursions there were the prelude to the launching of the main assault in the House of Commons and in Hooker's great treatise. The strategy of this double attack, involving the political front and the controversial front, was carefully planned by the clerical leaders in consultation with the lay leaders, chief among whom was Edwin Sandys, to coincide in time and so to increase the impact, as will appear. When the whole story is told it may be questioned whether Hooker was in all respects in harmony with his allies on the controversial ground which it was his function to defend on behalf of the Church. The most significant divergences, however, did not appear until a later date. It was, indeed, difficult to ensure a statement of the position of the Church which would meet with the approval of the varying shades of orthodox opinion in a rapidly developing institution. The first two instalments of Hooker's treatise, however, had little in them to impair the unity of front which it was necessary to present to the enemy. Books I to V alone were completed by Hooker before his death, and were printed during his lifetime. With their publication he had completed his main function in the great debate of the sixteenth century. And he had also laid foundations which outlasted his more immediate purposes.

Hooker's *Laws of Ecclesiastical Polity* is more than a magnificent piece of prose writing, more than a full statement of the views of a philosopher defending the position of the Church against its Puritan enemies. It is a document of Church history of the first importance, a manifesto to which the Church returns at every crisis to seek justification and vindication. When Keble edited the book, nearly half-way through the nineteenth century, his editorial zeal was fortified by his conviction that Hooker was on his side in the great movement which gave new life to his Church. It may well be that when Milton tackled the apologists of the Church of England in 1641, he found it easier to deal with the adversaries he chose, Andrewes and Usher, than with the judicious Hooker.

If the apologetics of the Church in Hooker's hands had been directed mainly against Puritan heresies, they had also been diverted from their original impulse derived from separation from Rome. John Fox could still, when Hooker was a schoolboy, write a zealous tract called *The Pope Confuted*, and the martyrs whose stories he related were the victims of the same adversary. Hooker's own master and first patron, Bishop Jewel, in writing his *Apology for the Church of England* in 1562, had in mind the Council of Trent then sitting, and his purpose was to vindicate the Church of England against Rome. But in later years he had no doubt of the outcome. In a sermon preached before the Queen he took for his text the story of Joshua and the walls of Jericho. The walls of the Roman Jericho were now down, and Jerusalem was built up in England on a firm foundation. Woe to those who sought to rebuild Jericho! He was content with the strength of his position as he set it forth. One thought only disturbed him—the old vanished fear replaced by a new dread. 'I am afraide of Printers,' he wrote to Parker on 3 May 1566, 'their tyrannie is terrible.' If only he could be sure that his writings would be properly printed!

For Hooker too the Roman field was won, and he had no wish to press his advantage. Indeed, in some measure Rome and Canterbury had now the same ground to defend. The rearguard action had become the capital affair of the Church. Jewel admitted into his polemics something of that intemperate animosity towards Rome which seems to betray surviving fear. But by 1588 the main danger was over, with the signal defeat of the Armada. And even if the occasion were still capable of arising, the nature of Hooker, alien to hatred, humane and tolerant, desirous of comprehension, professing and practising humility and charity, led him inevitably beyond controversy into exposition, building the mansion of God as he conceived its architecture upon deep foundations, assuming in his readers an equal measure of love of truth and of patience in search of it.

Some of those who read Hooker, indeed, accused him of Popery. Later Puritan opponents protested that his arguments would serve admirably for Catholic apologists, and were sent to prison for saying so in print. Walter Travers attacked him for his refusal to damn all Catholics, though Hooker's saving clauses, however kindly in spirit, are incredibly arrogant to a Catholic mind, in their suggestion that a repentant Cardinal, nay even a repentant Pope, is not necessarily a lost soul because he is a Cardinal or even a Pope, if only he repents. Yet it was a bold position to take up in days when Catholicism was treason as well as heresy, when extreme Puritans were only too ready to read Rome into Canterbury and Antichrist into both, and when Whitgift, Archbishop of Canterbury, was to the conventicles as plain a Beelzebub as the Bishop of Rome. Indeed, it is on record that Hooker was responsible for the conversion of James the Second to Catholicism, according to James' own statement. A further miracle, less alien to Hooker's true intentions, is recorded by Pepys. He came to hear about Hooker's *Polity* from his friend Chetwind, who reported upon it as 'the best book, and the only one that made him a Christian'. Chetwind seems to have run it fine, for he died only a year after. Fired by this report, Pepys determined to buy such a remarkable book. But another friend, Moore, no less aware of its miraculous virtue, and anxious for the safety of another valued soul, forestalled him and on 11 July 1661, twelve days after Chetwind's talk with Pepys, gave him a handsome copy. We may hope for the best, but Pepys makes no report upon the outcome. Six years later, however, Pepys was buying another copy of the book, in the new edition of 1666. We do not know what happened to his gift from Moore, which he does not seem to have retained. But the copy he bought may be seen in the Pepys collection in the library of Magdalene College, Cambridge. Pepys had it beautifully

bound in blue leather with gold tooling, some time after
the accession of James the Second, as we may see from the
inscription on the front which runs: *Sam. Pepys Car. et Jac.
Angl. Regib. a Secretis Admiraliae.* It bears his crest on both
back and front, and his motto on the back, taken from the
Somnium Scipionis: *Mens cujusque is est quisque*. One may
fear that whatever 'Hooker's Polity' did for Pepys may have
been undone by 'Hobbs's Leviathan', which he bought a
year later, paying thrice the published price for a second-hand
copy, 'it being a book the Bishops will not let be printed
again'.

The true purpose of Hooker's treatise was not, however,
evangelical. Its outstanding significance is political and
ecclesiastical. It is perhaps in its political foundations that it
meets with the readiest criticism.

> We hold, that…there is not any man of the Church of
> England but the same man is also a member of the common-
> wealth; nor any man a member of the commonwealth, which is
> not also of the Church of England.

Here was Hooker's answer to those who laid their foundations upon a difference between Commonwealth and Church
as two societies of different purpose, and of partly different
content. For Rome, the Pope is the Vicar of Christ, therefore
the sovereign cannot be head of the Church. With Geneva,
the Church ought to rule the State as God's kingdom upon
earth. With Canterbury and Hooker, the sovereign is head
of the Commonwealth and therefore of the Church which
is coextensive with it. Heresy was not only heresy; it was
sedition, a more serious matter in Tudor eyes.

The dilemma is obvious. Is there not to be one universal
Church of Christ among mankind? Then how can there be
one Church in many kingdoms, ruled over by many
sovereigns, each supreme within his kingdom? Hooker's
answer is to invoke international law, under which each
sovereign will take binding oaths; a kind of League of

Churches which will limit the practical supremacy of the individual sovereign. But it is a lame solution of a serious difficulty in his thesis.

There were bound to be other difficulties too, of course. Hooker was the nephew of John Hooker and the pupil of Reynoldes of Corpus Christi, and he had to overcome certain Puritan influences of his youth which led him for a time into errors concerning ecclesiastical polity

which so many have thought good to follow, and which myself did sometimes judge a great deal more probable than now I do.

There can be little doubt that we have here a reminiscence of the temporary exclusion of Reynoldes and of Hooker himself from their fellowships at Corpus Christi in 1579, when they opposed Warwick's nominee for the Presidency of the College, Dr Barfoot, an orthodox Church disciplinarian, their own candidate being Reynoldes himself. Hooker finds himself unable to blame altogether the French and the Scottish Churches, victims perhaps of circumstance, for

men oftentimes, without any fault of their own, may be driven to want that kind of polity or regiment which is best.

Over and over again he lays himself open to the charge of lukewarmness, a capital error in days of danger and intolerance. 'I am not hasty', he wrote, 'to apply sentences of condemnation', and again:

Let us beware, lest if we make too many wayes of denying Christ, wee scarce leaue any way for our selves truely and soundly to confesse him.

Walter Travers complained that Hooker acknowledged some partial truth and revelation even in the Catholic Church, quoting Hooker's words against him:

Thou holdest the foundation of Christian Faith, though it be but by a slender thread; thou holdest Christ, though but as by

the hem of his Garment; why shouldest thou not hope that
vertue may passe from Christ to saue thee?...bee of good cheere,
thou hast not to do with a captious Sophister, but with a mercifull
God, who will iustifie thee for that thou holdest, and not take
the aduantage of doubtfull construction to condemne thee.

And if this, he said, be an errour, I hold it willingly; for it is
the greatest comfort I have in this World, without which I would
not wish either to speake or to live. Thus far, being not to be
answered in it any more, he was bold to proceed: the absurditie
of which speech I need not to stand vpon. I think the like to this
and other such in this Sermon, and the rest of this matter hath
not beene heard in publike places within this Land since Queene
Maries dayes.

In general, Hooker's essentially kindly and tolerant spirit was
at odds with the conclusions to which he had committed
himself and with the cause which he was sustaining. For his
theory of the coextensive unity of Commonwealth and
Church was wholly incompatible with the existence of any
allowed nonconformity, and was a bar to toleration by the
State. The later seventeenth century tended to change its
stand upon this point. Hooker is certainly stiff enough on
the question of tolerating Catholic forms of worship as an
alternative: 'Tell us not...that if ye may have a Mass by
permission, we shall have a Communion with good leave
and liking.' He cannot 'brook to see a mingle-mangle', and
stands firm for unity in orthodoxy.

It was inevitable also that we should find Hooker laying
deeper and more constant stress on the main political questions of law and order to recommend his position than on
the fundamental ecclesiastical questions of the apostolic
succession and of the sacramental function of the priesthood,
questions on which Archbishop Laud later on took a much
higher stand. Yet it will appear, before the story now to be
told is finished, that the sacramental aspects of the Christian
life were much in his mind, and that Travers was not alone
in his suspicions of Hooker's Protestant orthodoxy. Part of
his treatise, indeed, it will now appear, was suppressed by his

own friends and advisers after his death, finding therein a savour of doubtful doctrine akin to Catholic heresies.

Finally, there was the thorny question of the alienation of Church lands during the Reformation. Hooker defends the dissolution of the monasteries by Henry the Eighth on the ground that their possessions were not in truth clerical property. But it makes queer reading when we turn to Archbishop Whitgift's solemn warning to Queen Elizabeth not to do it again, for now it would truly be a spoliation of a Church. Hooker, it would seem, was writing close to his brief here, under the expert legal guidance of Edwin Sandys, son of the Archbishop of York.

Such difficulties, and many more, were indeed inherent in the immeasurable scope of the debate which had rent England asunder once and was threatening, from a new quarter, to challenge the hard-earned unity of the Elizabethan settlement. 'For brethren turned enemies', wrote Jeremy Taylor when he fell heir to the problem, 'are ever the most implacable', as he came to realize most fully in the days of that later 'great storm, which hath dashed the vessel of the church all to pieces'. It is well to remember, not only the havoc wrought by successive persecutions under Henry, Edward, and Mary, by Catholic and Protestant alike, but also such words as those of the Puritan leader Cartwright in the very days of Hooker:

Heretics ought to be put to death *now*. . . . If this be bloody and extreme I am content to be so counted with the Holy Ghost.

And for Cartwright among heretics must be counted Hooker, Burleigh, and Elizabeth herself.

It is of the utmost significance, in the history of *The Laws of Ecclesiastical Polity*, that the publication of the first four Books of the treatise coincided closely in time with the passing of a Conventicle Act and with the execution of the Puritan dissenters Penry, Barrow and Greenwood. It may now be demonstrated beyond cavil that this simultaneity of action taken in the House of Commons with the publication of an authoritative book in defence of the principles at stake was intentional and was calculated.

With these considerations before us, we may the more readily understand the incalculable importance of Hooker's great treatise as a political and religious document of his own times. The full story of the circumstances of the birth of the book takes on an added interest. And we can realize the better the deep significance of the enquiries that were made after Hooker's death into the fate of that part of his work which was not printed in his lifetime. The Eighth Book, for example, was to deal with the vital question of the royal supremacy in the Church, as had been well known from the beginning. But only the first five Books had been printed before Hooker died in 1600. Here again the true story may now be told, in considerable detail, of the vicissitudes of Hooker's manuscripts, and once more the facts exculpate Mrs Hooker from the scandalous accusations perpetuated by Izaak Walton, in all good faith.

Our narrative, then, falls into three parts, all closely linked with each other. The circumstances of Hooker's life in London led him both into marriage with Joan Churchman and into the preparation and the writing of his great treatise. The publication of his work was a matter for careful calculation, in relation to political events, and moreover met with serious practical obstacles which had to be overcome. Here is a very exceptional instance in which bibliographical evidence may be checked by detailed external evidence bearing upon the history of the first and subsequent editions of a notable Elizabethan book. Finally, the disposal of the manuscript material left by Hooker at his death, material in particular for the unpublished Books VI to VIII, was entrusted to literary executors of the highest eminence and competence, with the fullest co-operation from his widow and her family. With this comes precious information bearing upon the history and the authenticity of Hooker's minor works, which were ultimately printed, after delays and negligences which seem strange to us to-day, from manuscripts which formed part of the same literary legacy.

§ iii. A NEW SOURCE OF MATERIAL: CHANCERY RECORDS

The records of the Court of Chancery, so rich in biographical information and still so little explored, furnish a mass of information which compels a restatement of most of the problems of interest no less to the bibliographer than to the biographer of Hooker. One might hardly expect *The Laws of Ecclesiastical Polity* to be a concern of Judges in Chancery, still less the circumstances of Hooker's lodging in London, least of all the destiny of the manuscripts he left behind him at his death. Yet upon all these matters legal debate took place, and evidence was adduced.

The principal new documents consist of a series of records of law-suits brought in the Court of Chancery, beginning about ten years after the death of Hooker, and arising out of the claims of his daughters as legatees under his will. The main precedent facts are these: Hooker died as Vicar of Bishopsbourne in Kent on 2 November 1600, having made his will on 26 October, and was buried there. His wife Joan, daughter of John Churchman, a London citizen, survived him, together with four daughters, Alice, Cicely, Jane and Margaret. His widow was appointed sole executrix of his will, and the estate amounted to £1092 in all. As overseers of his will he nominated his father-in-law, who also survived him, and his friend Edwin Sandys, afterwards Sir Edwin, of whom much will be heard later. Certain charitable legacies were made, and £100 left to each of the daughters, to be paid when each either married or reached the age of eighteen. The widow was made residuary legatee.

Mrs Hooker was married again not long after, to Edward Nethersole of Canterbury, described as 'Gentleman' in the record of the marriage in the parish register of Bishopsbourne, under the date 23 March 1601. Six months later she is found suing for unpaid tithe in the Archdeacon's Court, in her capacity as executrix of the late vicar. She left Bishopsbourne with her new husband for Canterbury, where she died two years later, and was buried there on 18 February 1603. Nethersole was then an Alderman of the city, and lived in the parish of St Mildred's.

It is to be borne in mind, also, that of *The Laws of Ecclesiastical Polity* Books I to IV had been printed, in 1594 according to Walton, the volume bearing no printed date, and having been registered in Stationers' Hall on 29 January 1593. In 1597 a further volume appeared, containing Book V. No more were printed in Hooker's lifetime. Both on the title-pages of these volumes, however, and in the entry in the Stationers' Register, the work is described as 'The Laws of Ecclesiastical Polity Eight Books'.

The Chancery suits in question bear principally upon two points: the legacies to Hooker's daughters, and the manuscripts of the last three Books of his great work, together with other manuscripts, as parts of the estate left by him to his widow and having interest, after her death, for his daughters. One of the daughters, Jane, is now dead, and the three who survive, being still unmarried and minors, are taking action through their kinsman and guardian, John Huntley, of Chipstead in Surrey, a Master of Arts of St John's College in Oxford. In all six suits were launched within a short time of each other, and ran their course in Chancery from January 1610 to April 1624. They were directed against various defendants. Robert Churchman, son of their grandfather and brother of their mother, had to reply to charges concerning the disposal of their legacies in money. Thomas Nethersole, the heir of Edward, had to answer for his dead father's neglect to pay what was due to the daughters under their mother's contract of marriage with him. Zachary Evans, husband of their step-sister Jane, Nethersole's daughter, was proceeded against separately on the same complaint, for his wife's share of Nethersole's estate should have been pre-empted to meet the debt to the girls. The statements made in the pleadings and the evidence adduced bear closely upon the family history of the Hookers, the Churchmans, and the Nethersoles. Sir Edwin Sandys is cited in respect of his failure to pay to Hooker's heirs their just share of the profits from the sale of his famous book, as also to answer in general for his stewardship as literary executor to their father.

Here the Court was inevitably led through a wilderness of testimony reflecting light upon the main issues from every conceivable angle. Whatever could even remotely bear upon the claims of the Hookers upon Sandys, or his efforts to balance such claims, was admitted in evidence. The intercourse of Sandys with Hooker, as collaborator, as guest, as literary agent, was subjected to financial enquiry. The history of the book itself, its origin, the circumstances of its publication, and all information that could help to draw up a profit and loss account upon the transaction, came before the Court. Finally, there was enquiry into the question of the remaining unpublished Books, and of manuscripts of other works left by Hooker and capable of profitable publication for the benefit of his daughters. As witnesses came friends of the family and friends of Sandys, servants of both, including Sandys' steward, Nicholas Eveleigh, a University dignitary deeply concerned in the whole history of the book and its aftermath, Dr John Spenser, and a famous bookseller, John Bill. The ground was very thoroughly covered. And few indeed are the questions left unanswered, even to the insatiable curiosity of the modern enquirer, when all the clues so generously strewn have been adequately followed up.

The last two suits, set on foot in 1623 and 1624, showed the plaintiffs now at odds with each other. Alice Hooker was now suing Huntley, her former guardian, for her share of Hooker's estate, which Huntley had received on her behalf.

Huntley replied in kind. He had, he said, maintained the daughters for six or seven years, and had spent great sums in law-suits on their affairs. And so the long litigation dried up, after fourteen years of debate, in the shallows of mutual recrimination.

Such is the new material available as documentary evidence upon all these problems. The full records in every case are not to be found, of course. Depositions are lacking where a Bill survives, and Decrees are not always traceable. In the most important suit, that in which Sandys is concerned, the Bill is unfortunately not before us, but happily there are two very full sets of depositions which amply make up for the loss.

With this new impetus to further examination of Walton's account of Hooker and his book, moreover, some fresh exploration of other sources of information became inevitable. The records of the Merchant Taylors' Company, for example, throw new light on Walton's story. It is a story which must now, in many respects, be seen to be untrustworthy, though nothing can take away the charm and grace of his narrative.

§ iv. HOOKER'S MARRIAGE

It may be that Mrs Hooker's second marriage, five months after her husband's death, played its part in the creation of what may now be described as the myth of Hooker's misalliance. Such a remarriage had been a very ancient theme of satire and cynical comment, from the Ephesian matron to King Hamlet's widow Gertrude, then appearing on the London stage. Walton makes great play with it: 'she stayed not a comely time to bewail her widowhood'. Yet it was a very difficult position for an Elizabethan woman of means to lack a protector for herself and for her daughters, a difficulty that is not so easy to realize to-day but is abundantly clear to anyone familiar with the intimacies of Elizabethan life. Bitterness, moreover, was bound to be engendered by the acrimonious contest in Chancery between the daughters and Sandys, and perpetuated in the memory of Sandys' group of friends, notably the Cranmers, who were Walton's informants. Sandys had done much for Hooker, whom he revered, and whose life's work was closely bound up with an issue which was the mainspring of Sandys' early public career. His reward from Hooker's own family was a humiliating financial inquisition. Mrs Hooker, it is true, was dead. And the daughters were minors, in the hands of John Huntley. But ill-will is no historian, and scandal revels in the thousand tongues of rumour and confusion, echoing over the eighty years that separate Hooker's marriage from its chronicle. As early as in 1618 Ben Jonson was telling Drummond that Hooker's children were 'beggars'.

The most vivid passages in Walton's *Life of Hooker*, describing the misfortune of his marriage, have long commanded the assent of history and the sympathy of readers. Hooker, it would seem, was inveigled into a most unsuitable marriage with the daughter of a London woollen-draper who had fallen into poverty and was paid to supply board and lodging to preachers appointed to deliver sermons at St Paul's, thus eking out an exiguous livelihood. Hooker, lodging there upon such an occasion, was persuaded by his diligent landlady that he needed a wife to cure him of colds.

Now the wife provided for him, was her daughter Joan, who brought him neither beauty nor portion,

and was moreover, in respect of character and temper,

like that wife's, which is by Solomon compared to 'a dripping house'.

She drew him, most unhappily, from his quiet College life in Oxford, and Hooker himself discussed with his pupil and friend George Cranmer the lessons to be drawn from 'his double share in the miseries of this life'. Finally, Walton dilates on his 'blessed bashfulness' and his short-sightedness, giving his readers full

liberty to believe, that his modesty and dim sight were some of the reasons why he trusted Mrs Churchman to choose his wife,

for he probably did not choose her himself. Such is the general picture. And with it goes the further story told in Walton's Appendix to the *Life* how Mrs Hooker allowed certain ministers (the implication is of Puritan persuasion) to intrude into Hooker's study after his death, and to burn and destroy many of his manuscripts; how she was sent for to London and examined by the Privy Council, made confession, and was found dead next morning in her lodging in King Street, Westminster. The whole story is common knowledge, a classical example of the private misfortunes of great men. Hooker deserved a true helpmate, a 'loving hind and pleasant roe', as Walton put it on his behalf. But he had Joan Churchman foisted upon him, 'a clownish silly woman and withal a Xantippe', as Anthony Wood phrased it in a later version of the story. And she was responsible, moreover, for the destruction of the last three books of the *Ecclesiastical Polity*. Better far if Hooker had gone on living in the wilderness or in the corner of the house-top, suffering from unrelieved colds brought on by that 'continual dropping in a very rainy day' to which Walton compares Mrs Hooker, quoting from the rich store of imagery in the *Book of Proverbs*.

On all the principal counts of this indictment Mrs Hooker must now be acquitted, and our conception of the general situation must be radically changed. Many of the statements of fact are inventions put upon Walton and innocently perpetuated by the old biographer in his last years.

Mrs Hooker's sudden death has already been disposed of by further knowledge. The story is impossible. We know that she lived on as Mrs Nethersole until 1603. Her home was with Nethersole, his son and daughters, and her own four daughters, in a house called Stone Hall in Wincheap in St Mildred's, Canterbury. But this is only a beginning. The date of the Bill in the first Chancery suit, in which the three surviving girls, Alice, Cicely and Margaret, sued Robert Churchman and Richard Stratford, is 25 January 1610, at which date none of the three have attained the age of twenty-one, for they are suing through their guardian John Huntley. The earliest possible date for the birth of any of the daughters is 26 January 1589. Now Walton puts the marriage of Hooker in the year 1581. Robert Churchman, again, brother of Mrs Hooker, was born in 1570, I find, for he gives his age when he appears as a witness in Court on 24 November 1613. He would therefore be eleven years of age in 1581. One wonders how old his sister would be in that year. Walton's story of Hooker being 'called to rock the Cradle', when Sandys and Cranmer called upon him at his vicarage at Drayton Beauchamp in 1584, must surely fall to the ground. None of the known children was yet born in that year. It is true enough that Hooker was presented to that living on 9 December 1584, but there is no sign whatever of his having taken up residence there. In September 1582 we know that he was still at Corpus Christi College, when the Mayor and Chamber of Exeter granted him a student's pension of four pounds a year. This vicarage was Hooker's first benefice, as far as our knowledge goes, and it seems to me that it was a mere stop-gap appointment, upon his departure from Corpus Christi, pending the success of efforts being made to gain for him the Mastership of the Temple. I have little doubt that he was an absentee parson, like so many others in his day, for the brief period of his incumbency of Drayton Beauchamp. His friend Edwin Sandys, for example, was incumbent of the Prebend of Wetwang in York from 1581 to 1602, and held the office during his Fellowship at Corpus and his subsequent career as student in the Middle Temple and as member of Parliament for Plympton in Devon. I take it for certain that Hooker was already in London in December

1584, pending his appointment to the Mastership in February 1585.

Some confirmation of this view may be found in an interesting letter in the Fullman manuscript collection in the archives of Corpus Christi College. George Bishop the printer is writing on 4 December 1584 from London to Dr Reynoldes at Corpus Christi, concerning the printing of some work of Reynoldes which Whitgift has refused to licence. In a postscript he informs Reynoldes that

Mr Hoker wolde neds have it goe unto my L. of Cant. otherwyse I was in mynde to doe it first,[1] which I wold I had done, that the world might have Judged of it, there wold have bin no talk furder then, yf it had bin extant.

Hooker was evidently in London early in December 1584. I do not think Bishop's letter can comfortably be interpreted to make Hooker merely Reynoldes' messenger to the printer. It might seem that in this event he would have had his instructions from Reynoldes. The letter suggests rather that Hooker was already settled in London, and acted in this matter as his colleague's agent, using his own discretion.

It was at this time, it would seem, that Hooker became a resident in John Churchman's house in Watling Street and, apparently, a permanent resident there. With all these facts before us, it would seem reasonable to conclude that the marriage was arranged during this residence, and took place in 1585 at the earliest, probably a year or two later. Fortunately, all doubts are set at rest by an entry recording the marriage in the parish register of the family church. Richard Hooker was in fact married to Joan Churchman in the parish church of St Augustine's, Watling Street, on 13 February 1588.

It seems reasonably certain that, after his appointment to the Mastership, and also after his marriage, Hooker continued to live, with his wife and his growing family, in Churchman's house. The parish records of St Augustine's announce the

---

[1] I.e. to print it without permission from the Archbishop.

baptism of three children in successive years, of a son Richard on 19 February 1589, and of two daughters, Alice on 10 May 1590 and Cicely on 21 April 1591. Then comes a gap of five years, until a second son Edwin was baptized on 21 June 1596.

It is true that there was a parsonage house within the Temple, but the indications are that it was not occupied by the Master. It was evidently in very bad repair, for when Hooker's successor, Dr Baldgay, came to the Temple, he was accommodated in 'Mr Candish's' chambers, and considerable sums were voted to make the parsonage habitable. Surely, if Hooker had wished to occupy it, we should have had earlier records of repairs. Possibly, indeed, the disrepair was due to the house lying vacant. We must remember, moreover, that part of the house was occupied by Walter Travers, Hooker's adversary and rival among the Templars, after Hooker's appointment, and probably during the whole time of his Mastership. Co-tenancy in such circumstances would have been embarrassing. Hector and Achilles could hardly be at ease together in the same tent. In 1596 the Temple ordered the continuance of Travers' salary as Lecturer and of his right to a lodging in the house till further notice. It might well seem that Hooker, the representative of the official Church, was considerably less in favour with the Templars than the jealous and censorious Genevan Travers, and that life, which Travers did all in his power to embitter for Hooker from the day of his first sermon in the Temple, was more comfortable for him elsewhere, particularly in Watling Street, where Churchman's house became the focus of the movement in defence of the Church. Edwin Sandys about the same time gave up his rooms in the Temple, and did not resume them until after the end of Hooker's Mastership, an appointment for which he was largely responsible, on 10 November 1591. One reason was that for some years during this time he also was a resident in Churchman's house, not as a lodger, but as a guest.

Walton's story bids us believe that Hooker, a Fellow of

Corpus Christi, came to London in 1581 to preach a sermon at St Paul's, lodged with Mrs Churchman for an unknown, but short, time, straightway married Joan Churchman, and returned to Corpus Christi for a further three years at least. It is fantastic. But it is not true.

I cannot answer the reproach that Joan Churchman was lacking in beauty. On this question there is no source of information other than Walton. But there is an alternative to Walton's explanation of Hooker's failure to disqualify her on this ground, if the reproach be true. And it is Hooker's own explanation. He does not invoke 'dim eyes', but the mystery of love. Writing of the sacrament of marriage, he bids us note how woman's natural inferiority to man is framed

in so due and sweete proportion, as being presented before our eyes, might bee sooner perceiued then defined, And euen herein doth lye the reason why that kind of loue, which is the perfectest ground of Wedlocke, is seldom able to yeeld any reason of it selfe.

Hooker might well have set up his Psalm against Walton's Proverbs, and surely considered the fruitful vine and the olive-branches around his table, when he set forth his views of marriage, whereby worship grows unto the wife, and a right of participation is given her both in him, and even in all things which are his.

The true story of Hooker's relations with the Churchman family can be told in part with certainty, and in part with a strong assurance of probability.

It is strange that no one has taken the trouble to enquire into the career of John Churchman himself, who is said by Walton to have been in 'a necessitous condition' in 1581, and to have kept what amounted to a lodging-house. Walton, it is true, gives him the credit of being 'a virtuous man', but leaves the reader to judge that his wife was a less desirable character. The facts are, indeed, startling.

Churchman, giving evidence in Chancery on 9 March 1594, gives his age as sixty. He was therefore, to the best of his memory, born about 1534. He was a member of a famous old family of Merchant Taylors, and the descendant of a fourteenth-century Master and benefactor of the Company. He married Alice Hulson, daughter of Robert Hulson, Master of the Company in 1569. In 1581, the year in which Walton describes him as fallen in estate, he was making his way to high office himself in the great Guild of which he was a member, being elected Third Warden. Eight years later, in 1589, a year at least after the marriage of his daughter Joan to Hooker, he was made First Warden. Finally, in 1594, about the time of the publication of the first four Books of *The Laws of Ecclesiastical Polity*, he reached the height of his ambition, when he became Master of the Merchant Taylors' Company, no mean honour, and an honour open only to a man of assured means as well as of the highest reputation among his fellows. It is pleasant to record that the Audit Dinner of his year of Mastership, for the first time in the history of the Company, regaled the guests with oysters, a delicacy provided by the generosity of the Master himself, Hooker's father-in-law. His probity and his standing were further recognized when he was elected City Chamberlain, an office of high financial responsibility and confidence.[1] It is beyond the bounds of possibility that such a man, in such a situation, should dismiss his daughter portionless. It was not the Elizabethan way of doing things, nor was it the way of a good London citizen, jealous of his own good name, honourably proud of what he himself would have called his 'ability', and of a generous disposition. Indeed, we now learn that if Hooker's estate at his death amounted to the considerable figure of nearly eleven hundred pounds, the greater part of it came to him with Joan Churchman. For her dowry amounted to seven hundred pounds. At Oxford Hooker was a poor scholar, and little, if anything, came to him from his own family. He held no rich livings, nor did his writings bring him profit, as will appear.

[1] But see Appendix D, p. 184, n. 1.

His marriage, in fact, was beyond question judicious, and we may believe that it was happy. It gave him an assured position, not only as the Master of the Temple, the friend of Edwin Sandys, and one in favour at Canterbury, but also as a member of the family circle of a great London citizen of wealth and civic rank. And his wife's dowry provided financial security for himself and his children.

For the beginning of these fortunate relations with the Churchmans we must consider probabilities. It is reasonably sure that they went back to 1581, the year of Hooker's sermon at St Paul's. It is likely enough that Hooker first became a guest of the family on that occasion. Churchman's house in Watling Street stood almost under the shadow of St Paul's. And there were bonds of union between Corpus Christi and the Guild of Merchant Taylors. Hooker's pupils and friends at Corpus Christi, Edwin Sandys and George Cranmer, went there from the Merchant Taylors' School. In 1581 Cranmer was a student at Corpus, and Sandys a Fellow of a year's standing. Sandys' mother was Cicely Wilford, sister of a Merchant Taylor. At Corpus Christi was a newly entered freshman, William Churchman, son of John Churchman, who died after two years at Oxford, during the Long Vacation of 1583.

Finally, it would seem that Sandys' father, when Bishop of London, resided in the same parish as Churchman, in St Augustine's, Watling Street. The records of the parish church chronicle the history of his family. There, on 19 May 1575, Margaret Sandys, sister of Sir Edwin, was married to Francis Evington, a Merchant Taylor, who subsequently had much to do with his brother-in-law. And there also, in 1581, the year of Hooker's sermon at St Paul's, a second sister, Agnes, was married to William Newcombe.

Here are links enough to explain Hooker's introduction to the family circle of the Churchmans, and to make him a welcome guest in the house in Watling Street, even apart from the fact that Hooker was coming to London to maintain at St Paul's the position of the Church against her enemies, a cause to which Churchman was as devoted as Sandys, as will appear. It can hardly be doubted that Sandys himself was responsible for Hooker's first acquaintance with the Churchmans, and for his first meeting with Joan and her mother. So the story takes on a different air, and a more familiar shape. A young Fellow and a Freshman of an Oxford College bring a senior Fellow of distinction, on a visit to London, into their hospitable circle of friends and relatives there. The admired guest soon comes to share this intimacy, and friendship ripens into a nearer relationship with the family of his host when that first hospitality is renewed some years later. A more suitable marriage could hardly be conceived. A strong bond of common interest in the welfare of the Church occupied the thoughts alike of the wealthy and respected London citizen and of the scholar and clergyman in whom great hopes were already rested.

Whence came then the circumstantial story of Hooker and his landlady, and the confident reference by Walton to the 'house of the Shunamite'? There is some evidence that this image may not have been merely an example of Walton's quaint turns of phrase and his allusive vividness of style. Richard Newcourt, for many years Registrar of the diocese of London, recorded in 1708, in his *Repertorium Ecclesiasticum Parochiale Londinense*, the organization of the sermons at St Paul's Cross, where they were preached every Sunday morning:

The Persons that are to preach these Sermons are from time to time appointed by the Bishop of London, and are chosen out of such as either have been or are of either of the Universities, by turn: They have usually about a Month's notice before; and had each of them 45s. as a Reward, and Four days Diet and Lodging, at the House of such Person as the Bishop did appoint, who is commonly call'd the Shunamite, who, for the same, was allow'd 15s. per Week. But the Preacher's Reward is now reduc'd to 35s. paid by the City, and 5s. by the Church.

Newcourt had the Registers of the diocese in his possession and at his command. And he studied them and used them. It would seem, on such authority, sufficient evidence of the origin of Walton's phrase. But doubts arise.

Newcourt is lavish with marginal notes citing his authorities, whether printed books or Bishop's Registers. He has, indeed, a historian's conscience in the matter. But no authority is given for these statements, though he had the Register for the period at his disposal. There is, again, a question of tenses in his statements, some clauses referring to the past and some to the present usage. The reference to the Shunamite's house is in the present tense, and may well signify a recent custom. Thirdly, the question may well be asked how it could come about that a lodging-house became known as 'the Shunamite's house'. For the story told in the *Book of Kings*[1] deals with no house of poverty reduced to living upon the fees of visitors or needing such a subsidy. The Shunamite who set a room apart for Elisha 'was a great woman', who 'constrained him to eat bread' whenever he passed by, and finally persuaded the holy man to be her guest. And when Elisha sought to repay her for her hospitality, she answered with pride, 'I dwell among my own people', and would have nothing of him, save later when the prophet's blessing brought the childless woman a son. These were days when people knew their Bible.

The Bible story had in fact a much closer analogy to such hospitality as the wealthy John Churchman and his wife might dispense to a visiting preacher from Oxford than to Walton's picture of a necessitous landlady. And we know for a certainty that it was John Churchman, future Master of the Merchant Taylors', whose daughter Hooker married in due course, and who was the husband of Hooker's Shunamite. May it not well be that such hospitality gave rise to, and passed on, a name and a phrase which at a later date continued to be used in respect of an arrangement for

[1] II Kings iv. 8–37.

preachers at St Paul's which had become an organized convenience, so that the name was no longer apt? Mrs Churchman, indeed, may have been the only true woman of Shunem.
So we may return to Newcourt's statement, in its precise
terms, that the person with whom the preacher lodged 'is
commonly call'd the Shunamite', in a phrase which had no
official genesis or authority other than an oral tradition from
days of more spacious hospitality.

But even these facts are only the beginning of the truth
of the matter of the 'house of the Shunamite'. When John
Huntley proceeded against Sandys in respect of what was
due by him to Hooker's daughters, he sought to argue that
John Churchman had been put to great expense by the
protracted stays of Sandys in his house. Very full and satisfactory evidence is brought in support of the contention,
especially by Philip Culme, who had been Churchman's
servant or accountant, and by Nicholas Eveleigh, formerly
Sandys' steward or agent, and also his brother-in-law, for
Sandys married Eveleigh's sister Margaret, unimpeachable
witnesses both. Sandys' sojournings with Churchman began
in 1588, after the death of his first wife, when he lived with
Churchman for two years, with one man to serve him.
When he married again, he returned to London, bringing
this time his wife, two men-servants and one maid-servant,
and all stayed with Churchman for a whole year. After the
death of his second wife, once more in London, he resumed
residence with his generous host for another year or more.
Robert Churchman, John's son, denies that any money was
paid to his father in respect of all this hospitality. Eveleigh
assured the Court that no question of money arose; none
was expected to arise; and certainly none was paid. And
Eveleigh kept Sandys' accounts. John Churchman himself
stated in Court, with some indignation, that he never
accounted Sandys his debtor for the hospitality he received,
that he never asked for any money, nor did he receive any.
One may imagine, from his attitude in Court in 1613, the

full measure of the resentment he would have felt against such an account of his housekeeping as that to be made current by Walton. It was bitter enough that his hospitality should have been made a pawn in a legal debate and used against his own friend and guest Edwin Sandys.

Even under the sordid pressure of such a debate, all that Sandys or his legal advisers could advance to set off against such unstinted bounty was the ungenerous plea that the friendship of Sandys had commercial value for a woollen-draper. Such a guest, it was urged, brought trade to Church-man's shop. And, in particular, upon the death of Archbishop Sandys in 1588, the order for mourning clothes, to the value of £200, was placed with him, to his great profit. Evidence upon this transaction was not elicited from old John Church-man himself, though he was available for examination. It might have been inconvenient. He was not the man to take advantage of dealings with his closest friends, especially when they arose out of so sad an event, the death of a revered intimate of his house. Sir Edwin, indeed, may well have been consulting the best interests of the estate which fell to him to administer, and to inherit. He cannot but be held responsible for any plea thus made. He was in London throughout the period of the suit, as a member of Parliament, a member of the Council for Virginia, and an active poli-tician. A good deal is said, it should be added, about the good will of Sandys towards Hooker's daughters in general, and in particular about his generosity towards one of them, Cicely, whom he placed for a time under the protection of his mother, the widow of the Archbishop. Old John Churchman did not hesitate to say in Court that Sandys did this at his own request, and that he took it as a great kindness on Sandys' part. (Churchman actually asked Sandys to take one of the girls into his own house.) Cicely was, after all, the godchild of the old lady, who was Cicely Wilford before she became Mrs Sandys. Sandys' vicarious generosity here may well have been no less a kindness to a lonely old mother.

Cicely Hooker is said to have married a Mr Chaloner of Chichester. The evidence cannot be confirmed, and there were many Hampshire Hookers. We may not at any rate attribute this service to Mrs Sandys, who died before any possible marriage of Cicely. She was a child of nine years of age when she was put in the care of her godmother, and we know that she was still unmarried in 1613. Some credit should perhaps go to Sandys himself, however. A letter from Hooker to Reynoldes informs us that Sandys was a neighbour of a Mr Chaloner. But it is clear that Hooker himself knew this Chaloner. His letter, by the way, was written from Enfield, when he was a guest for the time in Churchman's country house there.[1]

In reply to these somewhat nebulous entries on the credit side of Sandys' accounts, it was argued no less nebulously that he owed a great deal to Hooker's instruction in learning and in divinity. But there was nothing nebulous about old John Churchman's hospitality to Sandys as to Hooker, and it is not seriously brought into question.

The matter is touched upon in interrogatories put to their witnesses by both sides, it is true, but in respect of Sandys only. On Sandys' side the main point is whether Sandys could be said to owe Churchman for unpaid board and whether Churchman ever made demand for payment. The odd thing is that on the Hooker side a more specific question is put, whether Sandys paid ten shillings a week for board for himself and his man to Mrs Churchman, and this is denied by competent witnesses. It looks as if the Hookers were dealing with a rumour that had got abroad, and as if Sandys' advisers did not attempt to bring it into evidence, knowing that there was no support for it.

It will be observed that the amount in question is different

---

[1] Alice Hooker died unmarried at Chipstead in 1649. Huntley states that he negotiated a marriage for her with Thomas Langley, a London stationer, in 1618. She was then, he says, 'betrothed' to him. But the marriage did not take place.

from Newcourt's fifteen shillings provided for 'the Shunamite', and that it is in respect of Sandys, not Hooker. And yet this rumour, thus dealt with in Chancery, may be part of the origin of Walton's story, which owed so much to the Sandys-Cranmer group as authorities. There is little doubt that Sandys' relations with Mrs Alice Churchman were much less cordial than with her husband, and this is understandable.

There is an odd little story of trivial recriminations between Alice and Sandys, told by Robert Churchman. Alice and Sandys obviously had an altercation one day when Sandys was leaving at the end of one of his visits. Sandys replied to some complaint from Alice that at any rate he was leaving her house in better condition than he had found it, for he had provided and put upon a door a lock worth forty shillings. Alice was far from being satisfied. The lock was not worth more than five shillings, anyway. Her position clearly was that Sandys was being very grand about very little in response to so much hospitality.

After all, it was natural enough for Alice to look differently upon her husband's generosity. It was reasonable enough for her to see it as extravagant and tiresome for John Churchman to keep open house in this fashion. It is not always convenient for a housewife to have her house full of comparative strangers, and to have to provide dinners and suppers, very likely without warning, for their friends. Their servants were probably a great nuisance to her in the house. Her daughter and son-in-law were enough to have in the house, especially when their children began to arrive. And she had a considerable grown-up family of her own, all to be provided for in marriage. She could see the family money being wasted. It is an expensive business being Master of a great City Company, and more of it went that way, in 1594, in the middle of this period of visits from Sandys. After all, Sandys was not a poor man, far from it. In short, Churchman may have enjoyed doing things in a large way, with rewards in the shape of added importance, fine friends, and a share in a great project, literary, religious and political. But if Alice was a true Elizabethan woman, she was above all a mother and a housekeeper. And we can hardly blame her for looking askance at Sandys' frequent and long visits, apparently with a different wife each time! One may wonder whether, in considering the comforts of Thomas More's congenial life at Chelsea surrounded by a large circle of family and friends, we may not be apt to ignore the point of view of another Alice who is thought to have failed to appreciate her opportunities, 'a simple, ignorant woman, and somewhat worldly too', as Roper describes her in his large way. May we not imagine Alice Churchman addressing John Churchman some night, after a busy and weary day with too much ecclesiastical polity and its adjuncts,

Bone deus, bone deus, man, will this gear never be left?

And can we blame her? More too was generous-minded to a fault. When his barns and corn were burned, he bade his Dame Alice be comforted, for they might have lost even more, but was much concerned at any possible loss to his poor neighbours. Both More and Churchman were surely great trials to their respective Alices.

And just as Dame Alice suffered in reputation at the hands of Roper and Harpsfield, so did Alice Churchman at the hands of Sandys and Cranmer. We need hardly, indeed, look further afield for the real source of the legend of the Shunamitish woman.

It is abundantly evident that Churchman kept open house for Sandys, his family, and his servants; surely then also for Hooker too, at first for Sandys' sake, then for his own sake, as friend and son-in-law. And it seems as certain as anything could well be that the occasion for this prolonged and conspicuous hospitality was the preparing of plans for *The Laws of Ecclesiastical Polity*, and the writing of it, during which constant and protracted consultations were going on. Churchman's house in Watling Street was the birthplace of the project and the meeting-place for the consultants. We need not be surprised at this. Churchman was the friend of the famous Sir Richard Hilles, Master of his own Company in 1561, founder of the great Merchant Taylors' School, and a man of importance in the Reformation movement, corresponding with Bullinger, and carrying weight with his fellow-citizens of London in their attitude towards the settlement of the Church under Elizabeth. The zeal of such men for the New Learning allied itself naturally and inevitably with that view of religion which sought to base its polity and its dogmatic justification upon the rule of reason and learning, against the obscurantism of extreme Puritanism no less than against the authority of Rome. Where Hooker fought Travers on this point, as on others, Churchman was his ally. Not for nothing did John Churchman bear his surname.

Nor did his deep interest in Hooker's life-work end with Hooker's departure from his house to Bishopsbourne. We shall find both him and his son Robert intimately associated with the problems that arose, upon the death of Hooker, in connection with the publishing of his posthumous works, and in consultation with Sandys once more and with such notable persons as Dr John Spenser and Bishop Lancelot Andrewes. And so far there is no suggestion of any flaw in the prosperous and honoured career of the old Merchant Taylor.

When Hooker died in 1600, John Churchman was an old man of some sixty-six years of age. Some years later came the first signs of the coming eclipse which was to darken his fortunes, and which was to throw confusing reflections upon the memories of Walton's informants. That confusion, allied with some ill-will towards Mrs Hooker and, as we shall see, some theological odium, was the seed of truth out of which grew the amazing upas-tree of slander recorded in Walton's *Life*.

Towards the end of his life, John Churchman did in fact

fall upon evil times, and his fortune vanished. The Chancery suits under examination give the real facts about the decay of his estate, and Churchman himself reported them to the Court. His misfortunes, he said,

> grewe chefely by the greate losses which befell him during the late troubles in the Relme of Ireland,

and partly by the failure of ventures elsewhere. His son Robert Churchman confirmed his father's account of the matter, remarking ruefully that he also

> to well knoweth of the decay of Mr John Churchman in his estate and of the Cause therof, which hapned abowte nyne or ten yeres past,

that is, about 1604 or 1605. Robert's memory was accurate. And he is supported by certain Star Chamber proceedings. The long campaign of Mountjoy in Ireland, ending in the submission of O'Neill in 1603, had succeeded by dint of the complete devastation of the country by fire, sword, and starvation. Stocks were destroyed, contracts broken, and trade foundered in anarchy. The merchants in Ireland, who had taken delivery of large consignments of goods from London, found no market for them, and of necessity defaulted on their commitments. The London suppliers were left with worthless bills of exchange, nor could they obtain redress from Elizabeth. State Papers give details of the complaints and the claims of the Londoners. They had financed shipments to the huge amount of over twenty thousand pounds. John Churchman's share of this one venture was eleven hundred pounds, and Robert's eight hundred. Two thousand pounds was more than the two drapers could lose without approaching ruin. And the time came when it was evident that the Crown would leave them to face their loss.

By 1605 John's position was irretrievable. His fall was sudden and rapid. In 1597 he was still in a position to negotiate a handsome marriage for his second son, Robert,

with Anne Benyan of Coxhall, to present his country house
at Enfield with lands to the value of £40 a year as a jointure
for his daughter-in-law. Anne herself came with a dowry
of £500. In December 1604 he was reduced to selling his
house and shop in Watling Street to Sir Roger Jones, for
£700, to meet urgent debts. By January 1605 the old man
'began to keep his house', in the ominous Elizabethan phrase,
to avoid the service of writs for debt. In February he was
faced with a petition in bankruptcy, and a commission sat
on the 4th of the month to examine him and his son Robert,
with other witnesses. He was adjudged to be bankrupt, with
debts of £4000 and practically no assets. There were debts
due to him sufficient to meet all claims, but largely in Ireland
and irrecoverable. There were allegations that he had prepared for his bankruptcy by transferring assets to his sons
and by granting power of attorney to Robert. On the other
hand the procedure of the commissioners was not beyond
question, and their decisions were in effect left to the Puritan
Nicholas Fuller, who ruled that where any doubt existed
Robert's assets should be made available, to be on the safe
side! In the end Robert certainly kept his Enfield property,
after the whole matter had been tried in Star Chamber in
January 1606. The proceedings in Star Chamber add greatly
to our knowledge of the story.

What stands out most clearly is the respect in which
Churchman was held by his neighbours, creditors though
they were, and the grievous distress of the old man in this
shipwreck of his credit and probity. His creditors testified
to their 'good and reverent opinion' of John Churchman,
adding that they

did vse him as their father or brother,...some of them calling
him father and being redy as his Children & dere frends to travell
for him...without expecting any recompense.

Peter Bradshaw, the chief of his creditors, reports a con-
versation with John which expresses vividly how deeply the

old merchant felt his disgrace, crying out to the friend whom he had failed that

he was ashamed to looke any honest man on the face because he had delt soe badlie and dishonestlie with his lovinge neighbors, and wished that there were a lawe to take awaye his life for deallinge soe unhonestlye, and wished that he might be layed in some darke dungeon where he might never see honest man againe in the face.

He was over seventy years of age when this befell him. And it was the year in which another old man appeared in public in tragic guise—the year of *King Lear*, fallen from his high estate into wretchedness.

The records of the Merchant Taylors' Company perpetuate not only Churchman's former triumphs but his present distress. On 12 October 1605 the Company granted a pension to Churchman of twenty marks, raised to £20 on 16 December, the high rate of the pension indicating the esteem in which their past Master was held. And on 23 May 1610 he was elected almsman of the Company, with a lodging and with the same pension, a most generous scale of relief for the old citizen. There is no conceivable doubt that John Churchman, Master of the Company, and John Churchman, its almsman, as they appear in the records of the Company, are one and the same man. The evidence in Chancery and Star Chamber is conclusive. Such a tragic fall from prosperity to calamity was no uncommon spectacle in the uncertainty of contemporary commercial life. There was example enough for the fate of Shakespeare's Antonio in *The Merchant of Venice*. The poet Thomas Lodge had seen, in the career of his father, Sir Thomas, how even a Lord Mayor of London could fall into a debtor's prison, and be saved by charity. And the great printer and Grocer, Richard Grafton, ended his days in penury, a pensioner of his guild-brethren. The end of Churchman's pension came in 1617/18, and marks the year of the death of the old man.[1] But John Churchman continued in prosperity during the whole period of Hooker's relations with him and for some years after Hooker's death, the master of a great house in London and a country house in Enfield, and the dispenser of large hospitality.

The community of interests between Hooker and the Churchmans was in no way affected by Hooker's death. A notable solicitude was exhibited by Mrs Hooker for his children on her re-marriage. The marriage-contract with Nethersole bound him to double the legacy left them by Hooker. The dowry she brought with her was some £700, and she saw to it that more than half should be assured to the daughters and remain in Hooker's family. A bond to this effect was executed by Nethersole to John and Robert Churchman on 12 March 1601, and Nethersole also bound himself to maintain the girls until these monies were paid to them at the age of eighteen or until their marriage. Joan was still above all the mother of Hooker's children and the daughter of John Churchman.

Nethersole submitted to a hard bargain. But he was already considering how to overreach Joan and to evade her solicitude. The dowry itself could not be withheld from him. He used it at once to free his lands from encumbrances, conveyed them in trust for the benefit of his son Thomas by an earlier marriage, and made a deed of gift of other property for the benefit of two married daughters of his own. In due course he and his estate defaulted on the bonds whereby Joan had sought to assure the future. It is agreed on all sides that Joan's chief thought throughout was to provide protection and portions for the daughters of Hooker. The only unfavourable comment that is brought forward is a vague statement that she had dissipated some £100 of her estate during the interval before her re-marriage, and it is unsupported. In the end of

[1] The grant to Robert of the Beadleship of the Merchant Taylors' Company in 1621 was a further charity to the family. The son of a Master would not normally become Beadle to the Company.

the Chancery suit a compromise was arrived at with Nethersole's son that he should within five years pay £200, in view
of his reduced circumstances, instead of the £400 which was
to double Hooker's legacy. If he were ready to pay at once,
the sum of £150 was agreed upon.

The legacies themselves never came into Nethersole's
hands. When Hooker's estate was settled up they were paid
over in trust to the two Churchmans, father and son, who
entered into a bond of £800 to secure the £400, to two
friends of the family, persons of authority. One was Anthony
Stratford, a lawyer of distinction and, like Hooker, a son-in-
law of John Churchman. The other was Dr John Spenser,
subsequently President of Corpus Christi College, much
concerned with the publication of Hooker's posthumous
manuscripts, and evidently already in touch with the family
in 1600. He had married the sister of his schoolfellow George
Cranmer, Sandys' friend and Hooker's pupil. The Churchmans were to provide interest on the capital at the rate of
8 per cent, to be paid for the maintenance of the daughters,
who therefore brought into the Nethersole household what
was then the very comfortable sum of £32 a year.

When their mother died, in 1603, the children left
Nethersole's house in Canterbury and came to London to
stay in the house in Watling Street, in the charge of their
grandfather and uncle. They did not, however, stay long
with the Churchmans. The old citizen fell upon hard times,
and was stricken in years also, being now over seventy years
of age. Soon he no longer had a home to offer them. He
handed over the trust to his son Robert. Robert was also
anxious to be discharged of the trust, having cares enough
of his own. By March 1605 the girls were living with
Richard Stratford, brother of Anthony. They stayed with
him for two years, until March 1607. Thereafter John
Huntley took over their guardianship from Robert Churchman, and gave them a home with him at Deane House in
Chipstead, Surrey. By this time Cicely appears to have

rejoined her sisters, after her stay with her godmother, old Mrs Sandys, the date of whose death I have not been able to ascertain. So the care of Hooker's children in the end went back to old Mrs Churchman's family, for Huntley was her nephew, the son of her sister Ellen and cousin of Mrs Hooker. Huntley set to work upon the unravelling of all the financial complexities which he had taken over with his new wards, and his zeal led inevitably to a series of Chancery suits. It was Ellen who bore the heavy cost of all the litigation undertaken on behalf of Hooker's children, granddaughters of her sister Alice Churchman.

The Churchmans came well out of the enquiry concerning Hooker's legacy to his daughters. In 1613 the question was put directly to old John whether the legacy had been paid or not, and whether his own loss of fortune had not been a source of loss to them, through his inability to meet this claim. The old man of eighty painfully admitted the decay of his estate, but with pride went on to aver that his son Robert had taken up his burden and had paid in full. And it was the truth. Throughout the suit Robert asserted his anxiety to do the right thing at all costs. And all he did and said creates the strongest conviction of his honesty and sincerity. When, for example, his own counsel put to him the question whether John Huntley, the power behind all these suits, was not pursuing them contentiously and with ulterior motives, Robert's reply was that he verily thought that Huntley was doing it

for no other cause then only owte of the mere love that he bore to Rychard Hoker and the love he now bereth to his children.

In the particular suit against himself, he continued, he

could yet never lerne that he dyd yt owte of anye malyce or for any gaine to him self.

Long and weary wanderings over the contentious and unscrupulous levels of Elizabethan litigation bring but few such manifestations of a truly Christian spirit, such a spirit as John Milton's father once showed in a Chancery Court, when he spoke up for an erring apprentice of his who had robbed him, but whom he was willing to forgive, being but a young man, and to take him back into his service.

The question of the legacies had been settled in 1610. Robert's main concern was that, on payment of the money due, he should be freed of the bond into which he had entered, and discharged of his legal responsibilities. And so it was decreed, on 1 March. Robert had already paid £100, with no small difficulty. And within two years more he and Stratford managed to pay off the remaining £300 in full, together with £40 interest, Robert paying £200 and Stratford £140. A new trust was created. The trustee was now Francis Evington, a Merchant Taylor, a brother and former Master of John Churchman's Company, and husband of Sir Edwin Sandys' sister Margaret. So the end of it all is the knowledge that, despite the complete destruction of old Churchman's estate, he and his son stood honourably by their obligations to Hooker's daughters, and never wavered in their steadfast desire to meet them. When John Churchman saw how things were going with him, he did what he could to make some provision to help his son, who had shouldered the responsibility, to cope with it. It was an attitude that is rarely to be met with in these records, mainly the records of grasping chicanery and evasion.

Certainly it is contrasted with what we learn of the Nethersoles in these suits. Nethersole himself did all he could to defeat justice and to make nugatory all his own undertakings. Zachary Evans, the husband of one of his daughters, carried off assets of Nethersole's estate, and refused to give account. In the end he was adjudged to make restitution. William Dalby, a Merchant Taylor, who negotiated the marriage of Joan Hooker with Nethersole, told the story of Nethersole's plans to deceive his new wife and to defraud her daughters. Edward Weaver, who was then in Nethersole's service, confirmed this, adding that his master was disappointed in his hopes and expectations from her. It was from Weaver, too, that there came a side-light upon Nethersole's career which indicates how unfortunate was Joan Hooker in her second marriage, and which may even suggest a possible origin for the well-known story in Walton's *Life* about Hooker's blackmailers. Walton's story, though discursively dealt with, and fairly close in its essentials to that told by Gauden, is even more vague than Gauden's concerning essential facts. And it is a story that makes great demands even upon the most willing credulity. Weaver tells us in evidence in another Chancery suit that Nethersole had been committed to the Fleet Prison by the Court of Star Chamber in Easter 1607. He gives no further information.

It is true, in fact, that Nethersole was defendant in a Star Chamber suit in 1606. The proceedings are on record. The charge was perjury and forgery. A Southampton sea-captain, Francis Pettifer, had died. A relative of his, Nicholas Pettifer, a clergyman at Canterbury, with the help of his son and of Nethersole, had forged a deed after Pettifer's death, in 1598, dating it 1595. Nethersole drew up the deed, and young Pettifer forged the signature. In subsequent proceedings they all testified to this deed, in King's Bench and in Star Chamber, against the rightful heir, Ralph Robins. Now the forgery had been discovered, and a new suit was brought. The charge was sustained. Pettifer was adjudged to pay Robins heavy damages and costs. Weaver tells us that Nethersole was sent to prison, and another witness, Edmund Calton, that he was sentenced to the forfeiture of all his property to the King, a heavy penalty indeed. For such a man, the invention of irresponsible slander was in character. We know that he had expressed his bitter disappointment at the financial results of his capture of Hooker's widow. Her fortune was far below his expectations. Where had Hooker's money gone? The story told by Gauden was precisely such a story as Nethersole would have found most hurtful to his wife, most injurious to the memory of Hooker, and most savoury to the evil-minded. It besmirched Hooker, and turned his holiness into imbecility. It was the kind of horrible jest that acquaintance with the seamy side of Elizabethan England and with the painful prevalence of libel and slander in that period makes almost inevitable in the circumstances. And it lent itself to gradual elaboration. Mrs Hooker may well have let it be seen too clearly how much she had lost by her change of husbands. She had driven a hard bargain with Nethersole, to ensure that her estate should pass to her daughters. And she may have discovered that Nethersole was in desperate straits, not yet visible to the public eye. He was already, in fact, engaged in a criminal conspiracy for gain. And he married Joan for the use of her money. We cannot blame Joan too certainly for a bad choice. Nethersole was a man of good family and of great note in Canterbury, and there was as yet no sign of his corruption. He had been Mayor of Canterbury in 1590, as was his father before him, and was made Mayor again in 1604, after Joan's death.[1] The period of his greatness, as one of the chief and most respected citizens of no mean city, covers the period of his marriage to Joan. It would have been difficult for her, to all appearance, to have made a better choice for the safeguard and welfare of her children. Dearly indeed has her memory suffered from her association with her second husband, even if this be not the true origin of one particular piece of scandal perpetuated by Walton. But it is difficult to conceive any other source.

All the evidence of these suits points not only to the probity of the Churchmen, but also, and no less unmistakably, to the general love and reverence which all who were of his inner circle bore towards Richard Hooker. It is a theme that recurs again and again throughout these proceedings, more than ten years after his death. It is impossible to believe that his wife, Joan Churchman, was unique in her inability to

[1] I owe this information to Canon Shirley, Headmaster of the King's School.

understand what manner of man she had married. The facts tell against such a thought. And there would certainly have appeared some hint of it in these intimate records.

Of Hooker's four daughters one, Alice, was named after that Mrs Churchman who is treated in such cavalier fashion by Walton, and another, Cicely, after Sandys' mother, wife of Edwin Sandys, Archbishop of York. Mrs Alice Churchman, it might seem, was after all worthy to stand godmother to a child of Hooker, her grandchild, even alongside so great a lady as her gossip. The fact is that surely Hooker was most fortunate throughout his life in the loving and generous support, encouragement, and hospitality which surrounded him with even such a circle of friends and relatives as made Thomas More's life blessed. His own conception of marriage was of a high, holy, and happy relationship, and where he writes upon this theme he writes as one drawing upon experience. Surrounded as he was by a band of young children, he was unusually aware, and vividly aware, of the price to be paid in childbirth by a wife and mother. The joys of such a family life colour his thoughts of the religious life in the frequent imagery drawn from it in his sermons and his writings. 'Was there ever any father thus carefull to save his child from the flame?'—'that Father or Mother that rejoiceth to see the Offspring of their flesh grow like green and pleasant Plants'—'where should the frighted Child hide his head, but in the bosom of his loving Father?' But all was not joy.

For great sorrow fell upon Hooker in the death of his two hopeful sons, Richard and Edwin, whose births are on record among his blessings.

The hand of death soon took away these precious gifts. Both sons died in infancy, at John Churchman's country house at Enfield, hospitably open to Hooker and his family, where his daughter Jane was born in 1592. There died his first-born Richard, and was buried in February 1589, a few days after his christening at St Augustine's in London. In vain did the anxious father and grandfather send mother and infant, as soon as they could be moved, away from Watling Street to the purer air of Enfield. It was a sad sequel to the first anniversary of Hooker's wedding-day. There also died his second son Edwin, not long after he had reached his first birthday, and was buried on 22 July 1597. The blow was the more cruel for being repeated, and for being delayed during a year of hope and surely, towards the end, of prayer— 'Domine, descende priusquam moriatur filius meus'. Hooker did not complain. 'No', he wrote, 'God will have them that shall walk in light, to feel now and then what it is to sit in the shadow of death.' He was now at Bishopsbourne. And he spoke words from the pulpit there that his parishioners would understand and could hardly hear unmoved, as we cannot read them unmoved to-day. 'Can a mother forget her child?' he said, 'Surely, a mother will hardly forget her child.' Such sorrow must have bound husband and wife still closer together, when everything else points to community of interests and mutual esteem.[1]

It cannot be asserted that Joan Hooker may not have had a sharp tongue. She was an Elizabethan, after all. More's wife, Dame Alice, had a sharp tongue, and he was none the worse for it. But it can certainly be maintained that Walton or his informants seem to have got their names mixed. The true story of this marriage shows a Richard Hooker marrying the daughter of a good Churchman, not a good Richard Churchman struggling in the toils of two female Hookers. We may content ourselves with Hooker's own tribute in his will to 'my well-beloved wife', and 'my well-beloved father'. It is his own last word on the subject, and may well suffice.

[1] The choice of names and gossips for Hooker's children bears witness to the strength of the ties of family and friendship in his married life. To his first-born he gave his own name, and to his second son that of his friend Edwin Sandys. His eldest daughter was named after his mother-in-law, Cicely after Sandys' mother, Jane after Mrs Hooker herself, Margaret after Sandys' sister, wife of a friend of the family Francis Evington, Warden of the Merchant Taylors in 1608. There is a nice propriety in this order of precedence.

Chapter II

THE BIRTH OF
THE LAWS OF ECCLESIASTICAL POLITY

§i. THE WRITING OF THE BOOK

Hooker's great book was born under his father-in-law's roof. John Churchman's hospitable house in Watling Street was the common meeting-place for those with whom Hooker wished to consult in the planning and the writing of his *Laws of Ecclesiastical Polity*, and the scene of frequent discussions between Hooker and Edwin Sandys, George Cranmer, and Dr John Spenser. It was for this purpose that Sandys gratefully accepted Churchman's hospitality for a total period of some five years from 1588 onwards. And it seems almost certain that Hooker himself was living there permanently, with his wife, during the period of his Mastership of the Temple and thereafter, until his removal to Bishopsbourne. Even then, he paid frequent visits to his father-in-law in order to continue these consultations, during the later stages of the writing of the book. Eighteen months after Hooker's presentation to Bishopsbourne the baptism of his second son Edwin was registered at St Augustine's, Watling Street, on 21 June 1596.

Hooker ceased to be Master of the Temple in July 1591, when he exchanged benefices with Nicholas Baldgay, rector of Boscombe, Wiltshire, and was also appointed to the prebend of Netheravon attached to Salisbury Cathedral. There is no evidence on record of Hooker's presence either at Boscombe or at Salisbury. And there is every reason for believing that he held these benefices *in absentia*, even as he held that of Drayton Beauchamp pending his appointment to the Mastership of the Temple. Edwin Sandys, we may recall, at the age of twenty, still a student and not in orders, was a Prebendary of York Minster, and held his prebend, a mere sinecure, until 1602. Hooker was, after all, serving the Church in other ways, and the elastic conscience of his disposers, as well as his own more serious questionings, were amply satisfied. He has much to say on the subject himself, in Book v of the *Ecclesiastical Polity*, defending absenteeism or pluralism for those studying at the University, teaching there, or at the head of Colleges; for cathedral clergy; for chaplains to Bishops or at Court and even for chaplains to noblemen or to men of noble or gentle kin; and no less, to quote words which set forth precisely his own condition:

to men called away from their Cures and imployed in weightier business, either of the Church or Commonwealth, because to impose upon them a burthen which requireth their absence, and not to release them from the duty of Residence, were a kind of cruel and barbarous injustice.

The Church has laws which provide such permissions, and they are necessary; though Hooker is sadly aware of the abuse of such laws. But his own conscience is clear, on his premises.

We may fairly assume a reasonable certainty that Hooker continued to live in London with John Churchman, in Watling Street and at Enfield, and gave his whole time to the writing of the *Ecclesiastical Polity*, freed from the duties of an active cure and from the preoccupations of his controversy with Travers, until he removed to Bishopsbourne in January 1595 and became at last, and for the first time, a country parson with a cure of souls. His duties at the Temple had been those of a preacher, and the atmosphere there was not such as to give him scope for the exercise of his pastoral function among his flock.

Edwin Sandys was necessarily in London during various periods, from 1584 to 1586 as a law-student in the Temple during Hooker's Mastership, in 1586, and again in 1588 and in later years as a member of Parliament. It was during these later periods when Parliament was sitting that Sandys and Hooker shared the hospitality of Churchman and discussed the great question. Philip Culme, a man of some standing in Churchman's employ, stated specifically that both Hooker and Sandys were staying in Churchman's house at the time when the *Ecclesiastical Polity* was going through the press, presumably the first volume.

Sandys was a trained lawyer, learned in both civil and ecclesiastical law, and versed in the practices of parliamentary government. He therefore had much to contribute to complete the equipment of Hooker, whose training had lain rather in the history of the Church, in theology and divinity, and in the study of the Fathers. How far Hooker's other friend and pupil, George Cranmer, also shared in the work is less clear, but his contribution was surely of the same nature as Sandys'. Dr Spenser, like Hooker, was a divine. It would seem as if a team of four, two theologians and two lawyers, had formed something like a committee to draw up the general plan and trend of the book. We know that both Sandys and Cranmer were called in by Hooker to annotate the Sixth Book of the *Polity*, for we have to-day, in the library of Corpus Christi, the autograph manuscript of their notes, which must date before 1600. For Cranmer was killed in Ireland in that year. It was Sandys, beyond reasonable doubt, who pressed upon Hooker the need for the completion of his work for the press, or who conveyed to him pressure from higher sources. The occasion for this pressure in respect of the first instalment of Hooker's book was the approach of the great trial of strength in Parliament and the coming presentation of the Act against dissenters.

The first four Books were in fact written and made perfect, to Hooker's satisfaction, in time to serve their more immediate purpose. Before they could be sent to the Archbishop of Canterbury for his approval and for his licence to print, and before they came to the press, Hooker's manuscript had to be transcribed in a fair copy. So we learn from evidence given in Chancery. Information on this point is furnished by John and Robert Churchman, by Dr Spenser, and by Nicholas Eveleigh. In the words of John Churchman, 'the man that wrote out Mr Hooker's Books fair' was Benjamin Pullen, who was Churchman's servant at the time. Here is yet another link between the house in Watling Street and the writing of the *Ecclesiastical Polity*. The need for constant contact between Hooker and his scribe is obvious, to elucidate doubtful readings, to ensure accuracy, and to decide on lay-out. And here is also yet another service rendered by Churchman, in addition to his hospitality and his contribution of a well-dowered daughter, to his son-in-law, and to the cause to which both were attached.

Thus we now know for certain in whose hand was written that manuscript of the Fifth Book which has survived in Bodley's Library at Oxford, and which was the actual printer's copy for that Book, printed in 1597. The knowledge of this fact has further value, as will be seen later, in deciding upon the authenticity of certain letters of Hooker which have had doubts cast upon them. And this in turn has its bearings upon questions of literary style, in Hooker's more intimate manner. Pullen's transcription of Hooker's copy is a beautiful piece of clear and regular calligraphy, whether in his Secretary hand or in the Italic hand used for quotations. It is meticulously accurate, with few slips indeed, and it follows even Hooker's own spelling, as we may judge from a comparison of Pullen's spellings with Hooker's marginal notes. Hooker went over Pullen's copy carefully, making additional notes marginally, with occasional, rare corrections, and revising details of punctuation. The copy was such as to gladden a printer's heart. The result was a book, in the words of Mr Percy Simpson,[1] 'with a modest list of eight misprints—

---

[1] In his masterly book, *Proof-Reading in the Sixteenth, Seventeenth and Eighteenth Centuries*, in which this manuscript is described.

a wonderful tribute to both author and printer', and, one might add, to Benjamin Pullen too. There is no reason for doubting that the copy for Books I to IV had precisely the same history as that for Book V.

So then the first four Books were written, transcribed, and made ready for the press. There would be but little delay, one may imagine, in the granting of the approval of the Archbishop and his licence to print. He had been cognisant of the project from its beginning. Indeed, Hooker had in a measure taken over from Whitgift the task of presenting the case for the Church, which the Archbishop had maintained earlier on in his own controversial writings against Travers. The book had his blessing, as it had surely had the benefit of his counsel.

Yet at such a stage authors have often found that their real difficulties have only begun. A printer and a publisher have to be found. And even the judicious Hooker was not exempt from the common lot of mortals in this respect. On this unexpected point there is a considerable body of evidence. It is difficult for us to conceive that one of the world's masterpieces of literature in its kind could have so laboured a birth in print. But so it was.

§ii. THE CONTRACT FOR PRINTING

We have specific information from a distinguished stationer upon Hooker's negotiations with publishers, which took place in December 1592–January 1593. John Bill, one of the best known of booksellers of the time, who had been chosen by Sir Thomas Bodley at an early age to go book-hunting for him on the Continent when he was collecting for his library to be founded in Oxford University, was now, in January 1613 when he gave evidence, a man of thirty-seven. He related how Hooker offered his manuscript to several stationers, without success. It was perhaps typical that Hooker went straight to the Master of the Stationers' Company in 1593, William Norton. He was the most honoured man in his profession, had twice before been Master, as far back as in 1581, and again in 1586. Bill was his son's partner, and no doubt heard the story from him. Norton incidentally had his shop in St Paul's Churchyard, and it was but a step from Churchman's house in Watling Street. Norton refused to undertake the book, as did other publishers approached, 'for fear of loss', as Bill reported. Dr Spenser confirmed Bill's story, adding that the stationers to whom Hooker went with his manuscript refused to consider it unless Hooker would agree to contribute largely to the cost of printing. It was, of course, a proposal for a major publishing enterprise. Books I–IV made in themselves a considerable volume, and eight Books were envisaged. Hooker moreover probably explained the need for urgency in printing. An Elizabethan printer had no great capital at his back, nor had he any reserve of presses at his disposal. Such a proposal would probably mean the practical monopolizing of his presses, unless he were allowed to contract out for part of the work. And the publishers took the view that, whatever the importance of Hooker's book, there was little probability that it would be a profitable investment.

The reason the printers gave for their reluctance is interesting and significant; they demurred, we are told,

because bookes of that Argument and on that parte were not saleable.

That is to say, there was no market for books dealing with Church discipline in general, but particularly was this true of books written on the side of the established Church. There was more money then as now in the more exciting theme of opposition to law and order than in more conservative and orthodox activities, on the commercial side of literary production. The State Papers of the time bear witness to the uncontrollable demand for censored books in print. The products of the flying presses of the Marprelatists had in their time been snatched up avidly.

Nicholas Eveleigh in his evidence on the subject took the story a step further, explaining that

the Printers at that time were fearfull to adventure vppon printing bookes in that kynde for that the bookes of a reverent man being then newly printed were badly soulde.

Some printers, in fact, had recently been badly sold in an orthodox venture, and Hooker came in for the backwash of their unfortunate experience. I should like to be able to say that Dr Bridges' fourteen hundred page broadside was in their minds. But that was printed in 1587. Nor could it have been Bishop Bancroft's pair of books, *Dangerous Positions under Pretence of Reformation*, and *A Survey of the pretended holy Discipline*, both printed anonymously in 1593, for the *Survey* was not entered in the Stationers' Register until 5 March 1593, after Hooker's book had been entered.

There is every probability that the derelict publication which helped so much to frighten publishers off Hooker's book was a collection of sermons by Dr Henry Smith, which had been entered in the Stationers' Register on 23 September 1592, and was printed by a syndicate of three printers, Leake, Burby and Dexter. Dr Smith was a 'reverent man' in very high repute. He was the Lecturer at St Clement Danes, and according to Anthony Wood was famed as 'the Miracle and Wonder of his age, for his prodigious memory'. This work would have been 'then newly printed' when Hooker started negotiating, and none other can be found to fit the bill so well. Confirmation is to be found nine years later, in the records of the Court of the Stationers' Company, when Smith's *Sermons* were remaindered by Leake and Burby. They were left with a thousand copies of the book unsold on their hands. On 13 August 1599, upon their application, the Company permitted them to endeavour to dispose of this unsold stock by reducing the price to 1s. 8d. a copy. Dr Smith, a brilliant young divine, died not long after the publication of his sermons, in 1593, at the age of thirty-four.

It would be an unwarranted assumption that chagrin at the failure of his book contributed to his early demise, even as it was no doubt a mere coincidence that Norton died not long after the shock of confrontation with so vast and unremunerative a project as the publication of Hooker's series of volumes.

But there is no doubt that Hooker was deeply chagrined. Dr Spenser's evidence struck an intimate note, worthy of Izaak Walton, and added something that is of essential importance to any future biographer of Hooker. And here I turn Spenser's words into direct speech and modern form:

> I have long since credibly heard and do believe that Mr Richard Hooker having dealt with divers printers for the printing of his Books and finding none that would bear the charge of printing them unless himself would give somewhat towards the charge thereof, because books of that argument and on that part were not saleable, as they alleged, was very much dismayed, and that Sandys who was then daily conversant with him having at length fished out the cause of his melancholy did make him an offer to print them at his own charges and to give him a certain number of copies, which Sandys performed, with adding of certain monies, which offer Mr Hooker did accept very kindly.

No assistance was forthcoming, we are told, from 'the eminent persons whom the cause did most specially concern' and who sought to hasten the preparation and printing of the book for their own ends. And it is clear that the less eminent Edwin Sandys saved Hooker's *Ecclesiastical Polity* from suppression, by undertaking to finance its publication. So it is urged on his behalf in Chancery, and justly urged.

At the trial of the suit by Hooker's daughters against Sandys, a paper indenture was produced as an exhibit by his counsel. It was identified by Robert Churchman, Nicholas Eveleigh, and the stationer William Stansby, as the contract entered into by Sandys with the printer John Windet, and bearing the date 26 January 1593. It was the duplicate copy which had been preserved by Sandys. It was drawn up in Benjamin Pullen's handwriting, signed by Windet, and witnessed by Pullen and John Churchman.

We can well understand the choice of John Windet as printer for Hooker's book. It was all in the family, for one thing. Hooker and Windet called each other 'cousin', we are told. Windet was, in fact, the son of Hooker's aunt Anne, sister of his father, who married David Windet, an Exeter man, like Roger Hooker. It may be noted that the stationer William Stansby who appeared as a witness in this suit, and who succeeded to Windet's business when he gave it up, was also an Exeter man and started in life as Windet's apprentice. It is always well to remember the strong ties of local interest that bound together groups of Londoners from the same county, then as now. These Devonshire men were no exception to this general rule of clannishness.

Windet had won his spurs in the publication of works of theological interest, beginning in 1584 with Rogers' *English Creed*, and going on to *The Method of Mortification*, *The Glasse of Vainglory*, and *A Dialogue of Antichrist and Popery*, before he immortalized his craftsmanship with his cousin's great work, which is admirably printed. The venture was, moreover, a gilt-edged risk, on which he could not lose. We are, indeed, reasonably entitled to suppose that he allowed in his calculations for some profit to himself in the agreement entered into with Sandys.

The contract itself, which was produced in court, has not come down to us, unfortunately, along with the other records of the suit. It is not to be found among the Master's Papers as an exhibit. But some of the conditions are clearly stated in evidence, and they are the essential conditions. In particular we are told the terms on which Windet agreed to print the book. He contracted with Sandys for a flat rate of twenty shillings a sheet for printing, as Sandys' agent Eveleigh informed the Court.[1] Eveleigh himself actually

---

[1] This was in respect of Book v, printed in 1597, for which Eveleigh accounted in Sandys' absence. But it is clear that the contract covered the whole publication on the same terms.

completed payments on this basis for the printing of Book v, during Sandys' absence abroad in 1597. Sandys seems to have delayed his departure on his prolonged foreign sojourn with Cranmer until his parliamentary projects had been executed, and until the printing of Books i–iv of Hooker's book had been completed.

Books i–iv and Book v, in Windet's original edition, amounted to 53 and 72 sheets respectively, a total of 125 sheets in all. Sandys therefore paid over to Windet £125 in pursuance of his contract in respect of the printing of the book. There is no suggestion that Sandys, either himself, or after 1593 through his agent Eveleigh, did not fully and faithfully discharge his liability to Windet. A further point arises, of considerable financial import. It seems clear, on a careful examination of all available information, that Sandys' contract with Windet covered only the cost of printing and workmanship. The cost of the paper, to be supplied by Sandys to Windet, fell also upon him. We cannot, at this stage in our discussion, estimate this additional charge, but it may emerge later as an approximation.

It is of considerable interest to consider whether the contract was favourable to either party. Sandys, it is understood, was to have the disposal of the printed copies, and to recoup himself from sales. The edition was treated as his property. His right to do so was questioned in Court in 1613, but there is no doubt that in fact all financial interest in the publication passed to Sandys, as all financial responsibility was also his, and his alone. We may perhaps best consider the contract, in the first place, in the light merely of costs of production in an Elizabethan press. It is difficult to speak with certainty. But there are other transactions on record in the Court Minutes of the Stationers' Company which help us to come to some conclusion on this and on cognate questions which will arise.

The conditions on which a book familiarly known as Corderius' *Dialogues* was printed in July 1589 are sufficiently stated to give us an approximation, when we find out in addition the number of sheets making up the book. It was an octavo book. The type was pica roman, as for the *Ecclesiastical Polity*. The question of the cost of paper did not enter into the contract, which was concerned merely with printing and workmanship. A little calculation based upon the facts available shows that the printer was to be paid for setting up at the rate of 21*s.* per sheet composed, the price to include printing off and working generally.[1]

Now this transaction was one made between experts on both sides. It was a fairly exact parallel to that entered into by Windet and Sandys, except that both parties were stationers. The owners of the copy were the elder Harrison and Bishop. Robert Robinson was to print the book for them, on commission, and it was to be printed as their copy. And fresh editions, of 3000 each, were to be printed only when ordered by Harrison and Bishop. They supplied the paper and paid the cost of printing, and took the proceeds of all sales. The agreement was approved as just and proper by the Court of Assistants of the Company, a body of experts. It would seem, therefore, that Windet's terms to Sandys were eminently reasonable. It was in the main a matter of straightforward printing. But there was a vast amount of marginal matter, a great deal of Greek type was required, and even some Hebrew type. On the other hand, there was more workmanship involved in the *Dialogues* in certain respects, e.g. in folding. We may conclude that Sandys was fortunate in his dealings with Windet, and that some of the credit for the ultimate birth of Hooker's book, apart from its excellent workmanship, must go to its printer.

Sandys, after all, had his connections with Devonshire as well as Hooker, and Windet may have stretched a point in favour of the member of Parliament for Plympton as well as of his kinsman from Exeter.

[1] For details of this and other transactions on which this and subsequent arguments are based, see Appendix A.

Sandys' payments to Windet under his contract were, however, only the beginning of his commitments. He still had to provide and pay for the paper for the printing. This involved deciding not only the quality of the paper but the amount, which was determined by the number of copies printed. The normal number of copies printed of an Elizabethan book, setting aside grammars, catechisms, almanacks and the like, was 1200 to 1250. Indeed regulations were laid down in 1587 forbidding the exceeding of these numbers. It would probably be reasonable to assume an edition of 1200 copies. The greater the number, within the limits of saturation of the market, the better Sandys' chance of recouping himself. He was paying Windet 20s. a sheet, not so much a ream, for printing and working. On the other hand, the contract would certainly limit the number of copies, for Windet would not undertake to work an unlimited number of copies for his fixed charge of £53 for 53 sheets.

It is unfortunate that further details were not given in Court. But we may be sure that this is a true representation of the contract. Certainly we cannot interpret the arrangement to mean 20s. a sheet worked, obviously a ridiculous price. It means 20s. a sheet composed, the price to include subsequent working. This clause in the agreement was mentioned by Eveleigh, who stated that he himself paid Windet at this rate, on behalf of Sandys, in respect of Book v, printed in 1597. But it is quite clear that the one contract covered the whole project, which contemplated eight books from the beginning.

The price of the paper supplied by Sandys may be taken as not less than 7s. per ream. When Peter Short contracted to complete the printing of Fox's *Book of Martyrs* in 1589, four years earlier, this was the rate fixed by the Stationers' Company. Short's contract for paper was on a much larger scale, approximately eight to ten times as large as that of Sandys. And the paper actually provided for the *Polity* is notably superior to that used for Short's *Book of Martyrs*. Sandys probably deputed Windet to be his buying agent for the paper. And the price was probably 7s. 6d. to 8s. the ream.

Sandys therefore made himself responsible for very considerable obligations under his contract with Windet. The cost of printing and workmanship amounted to a total of £125 for the two volumes printed. The paper actually used, with no allowance for spoils, amounted to a total of 150,000 sheets for the 1200 copies. With the ream at 500 sheets, we have 300 reams at the rate of 7s. 6d. the ream, costing £112. 10s. 0d. In all Sandys had thus to provide £237. 10s. 0d. It will be noted that the cost of printing here works out slightly higher than that of the paper, though it has generally been held that the cost of paper was probably the greater item in the finance of an Elizabethan book. It may also be observed that the total cost in respect of Books I–IV was £100. 14s. 0d., and in respect of Book V, £136. 16s. 0d. This will be of interest when we come to consider the sale-price and Sandys' balance-sheet.

It was, then, on these terms that Sandys arranged for the publication of Hooker's *Ecclesiastical Polity*, upon a contract with Windet signed on 26 January 1593. It was evidently agreed that Windet was also to undertake the actual selling of the books and to account for sales to Sandys. This is made clear, in the first place, by the title-page of the first edition:

Printed at London by Iohn Windet, dwelling at the signe of the Crosse keyes near Powles Wharffe, and are there to be soulde.

The last six words are printed in bolder type. Paul's Wharf was perhaps a less accessible and less popular district than Paul's Churchyard for book-buyers. And in any case Windet arranged for other booksellers, John Bill in particular, to take over parts of the edition to be sold on commission.

Nicholas Eveleigh is our authority for the statement that he himself in 1597 received from Windet, during Sandys' absence abroad, sums of money in respect of sales of copies of Book v, recently printed, and also of arrears of sales of Books I–IV. Copies of the first volume, it seems, were still being sold in 1597, and the edition was not exhausted. The question of the success or failure of the book in the market will be considered later, and the enquiry will invoke bibliographical evidence as well as the evidence of witnesses in Court. In the ordinary way, it would not seem wise to entrust the distribution and selling of a book printed on commission to the printer, if he has no interest in the proceeds. But we do not know whether the contract made provision for such an interest or not. And in any case Windet was interested in further instalments of the work, and was personally interested in the success of the book and of its author, his cousin Hooker.

Sandys' payments to Windet for the actual printing, and his purchase of the paper, did not however exhaust his liabilities. There was Hooker to be considered. There does not seem to have been any legal contract between Hooker and Sandys. There is general agreement among the witnesses that the copy for the *Ecclesiastical Polity* was conveyed by Hooker to Sandys, and that this transfer of copyright to him was to cover the whole work in eight Books. But it is clear that this was only an understanding between Hooker and Sandys, and that no indenture of conveyance was executed, or even contemplated. It was, indeed, in the conditions of the law and of the publishing trade at the time, an impossible transaction as between the two men. There was no legal property to be conveyed. All Hooker could do was to hand over to Sandys the actual manuscript of his work. And it was agreed that Sandys should pay Hooker for it.

Sandys was to pay him £40 or £50 for the whole work in eight Books, and in addition was to present him with a number of free copies of the printed work as it came out in instalments. The number of copies is nowhere stated. The copy was to be paid for in instalments, as Hooker perfected it and gave it to Sandys for printing. Eveleigh, who kept

Sandys' accounts, reported that Sandys actually paid Hooker £10 for the copy for the first four Books, and promised a further £40 for the remainder. In fact, he paid £20 on receiving the copy for Book v, and paid no more pending the completion and publication of Books vi–viii,

forbearing to pay the other xx^{li} till the later bookes should be published.

Dr Spenser confirmed the payment of £20 to Hooker for Book v. And Eveleigh stated precisely that this Book finished printing in December 1597.

We have therefore to add these payments to Sandys' burden, and to the cost of the two volumes published, making a total of £267. 10s. 0d. actually expended. The cost to him of Books i–iv was thus £110. 14s. 0d., and of Book v £156. 16s. 0d.

Sandys, in fact, sank a great deal of money in the venture, the equivalent perhaps of £1500 to-day. And it was a very precarious investment, quite apart from the problematic fate of the book in the market. For Sandys had no assured property in the copy purchased from Hooker and printed by Windet at his expense. When the book was registered in Stationers' Hall, it was entered there as John Windet's copy, in spite of the fact that Sandys had bought and paid for it. Windet, in fact, was the owner of the sole effective right in the copy for the book, and this entry assured it to him. This was inevitable, for the Stationers' Company assured copyright only to its own members by such entries. This was, of course, one of the difficulties of Sandys' position, and later on it became manifest, and affected the financial success of his venture. When William Stansby, Windet's apprentice and subsequently his successor, came into possession of Windet's business, he took it for granted that he had an absolute right to the copy of the *Ecclesiastical Polity*, Books i–v, along with other books belonging to Windet, and proceeded to print it when he thought fit, for his own undivided profit. He had the full authority of the Stationers' Company in taking this view. The copy had been registered as Windet's, and had not been transferred to any other stationer. Stansby's position was impregnable. But Windet, fortunately for Sandys, kept to the spirit of his agreement as long as he lived, and this too may fairly be recorded to the credit of Hooker's printer-cousin.

§ iii. THE DATE OF THE FIRST EDITION

The printing-contract was signed on 26 January 1593. The manuscript of the first four Books was evidently in the hands of the Archbishop of Canterbury, awaiting his licence for publication, or had more likely already been returned from him, duly licensed. Three days later, on 29 January, the book was approved and entered to Windet in the Stationers' Register. Sandys and Windet were agreed and ready to fulfil their contract for the printing. Nothing stood in the way of the book going to press. And the political situation urged immediate publication. The question is whether it was printed at once or not.

The first edition of the first four Books bears no date on its title-page. Walton gives his authority for 1594 as the date of publication, and this date has been universally accepted hitherto, except by a recent writer. Mr Houk,[1] in his study of the Eighth Book, argues from internal evidence in the Preface to the first edition of Books I–IV that the Preface must have been written and set up before 25 March 1593, and that the actual printing of the edition must have preceded the end of the year 1593 in the old style, before 25 March 1594. He justly points to the entry in Andrew Maunsell's *Catalogue of English printed books*, printed in 1595 by John Windet, which records Hooker's book as 'Printed by John Windet, 1593, in folio'. He suggests, however, that

---

[1] Raymond Aaron Houk, *Hooker's Ecclesiastical Polity Book VIII.* Columbia University Press, 1931.

the book was withheld from general publication for some time, though available in limited circulation—a very difficult theory.

He thus accepts the traditional reason for delay in publication, namely the well-known letter from Hooker to Burleigh, quoted in Strype's *Life of Whitgift*, ending with the sentence:

> Wherefore submitting both myself and these my simple doings unto your Lordship's most wise judgment, I here humbly take my leave.
>
> London, the xiiith of March 1592 (i.e. 1593).

Strype quotes the letter under the heading

> Mr Richard Hooker to the Lord Treasurer, when he sent him the written copy of his Ecclesiastical Polity,

and Mr Houk, like everyone else, accepts the view that Hooker was sending the manuscript to Burleigh, and that therefore the book did not proceed to publication until Burleigh sent the manuscript back with his approval, some time after 13 March 1593. The theory seems exceedingly improbable, more improbable than the usual and simpler conception of similar delay in going to press. It is to be noted that Mr Houk accepts also the general view that the manuscript sent to Burleigh comprised all eight Books, fully written and ready for the press. Indeed, it is essential to his thesis. And he suggests that, while Books I–IV could hardly offend Burleigh, it was far otherwise with Books VI–VIII, and that Hooker consequently was led of necessity to fundamental revision of these Books. Setting aside this part of the theory, we may consider it in reference to Books I–IV and to the first edition of the volume.

What manuscript copy went to Burleigh, in the first place? It could hardly have been Hooker's rough draft. We know that his drafts had to be copied out fair by Pullen. And we hear something about Hooker's way of writing his drafts, on 'scattered pieces of paper'. It is unthinkable. But the alternative is almost worse. There was the fair copy made by Pullen. But this had already been to Archbishop Whitgift and bore his licence under his own hand. And thereafter it had been presented by Windet in Stationers' Hall for entry and duly entered. This copy was in Windet's hands, together with a contract for its printing. Why should it have lain with Windet for two months, and then suddenly be taken from him, handed back, not to Sandys but to Hooker, and thus by devious ways sent to Burleigh in a belated after-thought for his approval? Why was his approval not sought before the sponsors of the book had proceeded so far? Why was his approval the last to be sought? What would Burleigh have said when he saw Whitgift's approving sign-manual on the manuscript on which he was asked to give his decision? And what would Whitgift have said if Burleigh had set his veto against the Archbishop's own sanction and approval in a matter so close to his heart? This was his business, not the Lord Treasurer's, and he had said his say. Nay more, he was pressing for speed and expedition.

On ecclesiastical matters Whitgift tolerated no dictation. There had been trials of strength already, even in relation to Hooker and his work. Walter Travers had been tutor to Burleigh's son, and was supported by his patron as a candidate for the Mastership of the Temple. But the Archbishop spiked his guns by a letter to the Queen, and his brother of York put forward Hooker, who was appointed. Burleigh backed Travers' petition to the Privy Council against Whitgift, but Whitgift had him silenced none the less. The submission of the *Ecclesiastical Polity* after this fashion to Burleigh was unthinkable; it would be difficult to imagine a proceeding fraught with more explosive possibilities.

The fact is that there is nothing in the letter to support the notion. The letter, on the contrary, bears the clearest signs that it is not sought to obtain Burleigh's sanction, but that a present is being sent to him. Hooker is sending him his writings because that which moves me so to do, is a dutiful affection some way to manifest itself, and glad to take this present occasion, for want of other more worthy your Lordship's acceptation.

Surely these words are decisive. An occasion has arisen permitting Hooker to show his affection and duty to one of the pillars of the State, and he sends a gift which he prays Burleigh to accept. The 'present occasion' is the completion of the printing of his great work in its first instalment. Hooker has just received from Sandys or Windet his complimentary copies, fresh from the press, not without some excitement and joy. It was the first time he had seen his name and his work in print. It was a beautiful book. And its significance went beyond even its own merits, for great matters were at stake.

So Hooker sat down to write his letter to Burleigh, and with it went one of his cherished copies duly inscribed, just as Whitgift sent to Burleigh a copy of his *Defence of the Answer to the Admonition*. Hooker's 'over-boldness' and his 'fault', of which he writes to Burleigh, lie not in writing the *Ecclesiastical Polity*, but in venturing to obtrude himself upon the great man with his 'poor and slender labours'. These are commonplaces of Elizabethan dedications and compliments. Shakespeare, for example, would have understood this letter perfectly, and at once, as a parallel to his own expressions of duty and apologies for unworthy manifestations of it, in 'unpolished lines'. It would have been a greater fault, Hooker goes on, if he had not at once submitted his book to Burleigh for approbation 'with the first', that is 'among the first'. For Burleigh is a mainstay of law in England, and the chief servant of the Queen. But neither Hooker nor Whitgift would have submitted the writing and printing of this book, and with it the cause of episcopacy and conformity, to the censorship of Burleigh, once its opponent and never more than lukewarm. Hooker may, indeed, have had some hope of converting Burleigh's Laodicean error to the zeal of the true faith by the arguments of his book.

The fact is, therefore, that Hooker's letter to Burleigh proves that the manuscript had gone straight to press after the contract was signed and the copy registered, and that printing was finished before 13 March 1593, in the space of one and a half months. It was admirably timed for the debate on the question in the House of Commons which preceded the re-affirmation of an Act enforcing conformity and now specifically widened and strengthened to deal with dissenters as well as Catholics. Precisely on 13 March 1593, the very day on which Hooker sent one of the first copies of his book to Burleigh with an accompanying letter, Edwin Sandys made a speech on the bill before Parliament, attacking Brownists and Barrowists, and demanding their inclusion in its provisions. Next day, on 14 March, the bill was handed over to Burleigh to go to Committee. And the Lord Treasurer now had the advantage of being able to consider its clauses in the light of the new and important book awaiting him in his study. He did not need to read far. For Hooker plunged at once, in his Preface, into the very root of the matter then before Parliament, and before Burleigh, for it deals with the errors of the Puritan dissenters. Their innovations are dangerous, tending to anarchy, and posterity may well be the sufferer. And, the Preface ends, 'with us contentions are now at their highest float'. It is above all things necessary to establish peace and law.

The year 1593 records two milestones in the history of the Church, the passing of the 'Act to retain the Queen's subjects in their due obedience', and the publication of Hooker's *Ecclesiastical Polity*, and both in the same month.

If this account of the actual printing of the *Ecclesiastical Polity*, Books I–IV, in its first edition is supported by the evidence examined, it must nevertheless be considered in the light of technical considerations. For it would appear that fifty-three sheets were set up, proofed, printed off, and perfected, all within the space of one and a half months, between 29 January and 13 March. If so, it was no mean feat. But it was not in the least impossible. The copy was exceptionally perfect and clear, the equivalent of a printed text. Windet, we know, had three presses, and was well supplied with type. The productions of his press, not least this particular book, testify to the quality of his workmen. It is most probable that the printing of the *Polity* monopolized his press during the period of its production. There is no indication in the Stationers' Register of any other copy being entered by Windet during this time.[1] And there was always the possibility of putting out to another printer any other necessary work. The *Polity* itself was certainly printed wholly by him. We know, moreover, that pressure was brought to bear upon all concerned to hasten publication.

Peter Short finished his part of the *Book of Martyrs* in June 1596, in fourteen months or less, and had eight to ten times the amount of printing involved in the *Polity* to cope with, as well as a great number of illustrations. Newbury's *Decades* bears the date 1587, and was completed within a year, with its 155 sheets, three times the amount of the *Polity*. Neither of these was a matter of urgency. Finally, we cannot help noting that Books I–IV, in Windet's edition, show 31 misprints of some importance in 53 sheets of print, as compared with the eight misprints of his 1597 edition of Book V, in 72 sheets. His copy, we know, was of the same high quality, in the same hand, in both cases. The suggestion is obvious that the reason for this disparity was more rapid printing in 1593.

Confirmation of this date may be found in a copy of the first edition of Books I–IV now in the library of University College, London. On its title-page it bears the name of its first purchaser and possessor, Edward Pytt, whom I have identified as Sir Edward Pytt, Lord of the Manor of Kyre Wyard in Worcestershire, who died there on 11 January

---

[1] There is no entry to Windet, except Hooker's book, between 6 March 1592 (Powell's *Assise of Bread*) and 21 March 1593 (*Defensative against the Plague*). Indeed, the date of this last entry, just a week after the first copies of the *Polity* went to Hooker, strengthens the case.

1618. He was an officer of the Court of Common Pleas, and a Fellow of the Inner Temple. He would necessarily be in London during the law-terms, and was evidently a man of reading. A number of his books came into the market in 1933, including the Hooker volume, Rastell's *Statutes* of 1579, and North's *Dial of Princes* of 1568. He was apparently a methodical buyer, and not only wrote his name on his books, but also noted in ink the date of purchase and the price he paid. The date marked is 1593. The price marked is three shillings.

§iv. THE BOOK AND THE BOOK-TRADE

There is ample evidence in the Chancery documents on the question of price, as on all questions concerning the fate of the printed book in the book-trade. Statements were made by most of the witnesses called, including John Bill, who had a hand in most considerable transactions in books, as well as in the purchase of books for Bodley's Library in particular. Bill had entered into some arrangement with Sandys, it would seem, to share in the selling of the 1597 edition of Book v, and remaining copies of Books I–IV, on Bill's return from the Continent. He was unfortunately not informative on the conditions of his share in the selling, except to say that he never took over the sale of a whole 'impression' or edition. But he tells us what price was set by Sandys for retail selling, and it would seem clear that he sold the book on commission. Up to 1597, it seems, Windet had been bookseller as well as printer. Thus Books I–IV were on sale at Windet's own shop on Paul's Wharf. There was nothing, of course, to prevent any bookseller buying a few copies from Windet and selling them at a profit, and there is evidence of one such transaction in respect of Books I–IV.

Windet's former apprentice, William Stansby, reported that Windet sold Books I–IV for 2s. 6d. and Book v for 3s. Bill confirmed these as the prices set by Sandys; at any rate this was all that had to be accounted for by him to Sandys for any copies sold. Bill also stated that Sandys agreed that he should sell the two volumes together, Books I–V, for 6s. 6d., thus allowing Bill a margin of profit of a shilling on each set. It is evident that the sale of the two volumes together, after 1597, was a frequent occurrence, the old sheets of 1593 being sold with the new 1597 sheets. All but one of the copies of the first edition of the book which I have seen contain both volumes sewn together. There is a copy in the British Museum which shows clearly, in its present condition, the contemporary thongs binding together the sheets of each part separately as well as those uniting the whole set. The University College copy is the exception, and the probable history of its purchase and removal to Worcestershire furnishes the explanation.

Bill's actual sales, he told the Court, were made at varying prices, ranging from 6s. to 6s. 8d. And he complained that another bookseller asked, and got, ten shillings for a copy! Nicholas Eveleigh, who kept Sandys' accounts, and took the receipts from the sale of the book, also recorded the price of Books I–IV as 2s. 6d. When Sir Edward Pytt bought his copy of the first four Books in 1593, some bookseller obviously took a sixpenny profit on the sale, practically the same rate of profit as that allowed by Sandys to Bill, that is, about 20 per cent. These transactions, of course, relate to the book in sheets, unbound, according to the usual practice. The binding of a book was a separate, subsequent transaction.

It was argued in Court, on behalf of Hooker's children, that the sale of the book had been hindered by Sandys seeking too great profit and in pursuance of this setting too high prices for the market. Hence, the argument continued, profits were in fact lost which might have come in part to the children. It is certain that Hooker himself had some say in the matter. He was anxious to keep the price as low as possible, as Sandys himself told Robert Churchman. And

Hooker's desires carried some weight, as Eveleigh informed the Court:

wheras I and the printer had purposed to sell the fift booke for iij^s vj^d, Mr Hooker vppon some Complaynte made to him by some of the Company of the Stationers dyd will and order that the Vth booke should be sould for iij^s and rather then the booke should be sould derer, semed Contented to lose the benefyt which was promised to him for his paynes.

It would seem then that Windet had discussed the question of the price of Book v with Sandys' agent, and had agreed with him on the price of 3s. 6d. The Stationers' Company, or rather some of its members, intervened by approaching Hooker himself, who showed great good will, even to the extent of offering to forego the payment of £20 due to him from Sandys for the copy, as author. It was obviously Hooker's desire to extend the sale and influence of the book at all costs. For him its publication was not a commercial transaction; it was a crusade.

Once more Hooker's character and spirit ring true and clear. And it may seem also that both Sandys and Windet may equally be applauded, especially Sandys, whose sole financial responsibility it was. Yet he yielded to Hooker's 'will and order', with befitting deference. For surely letters passed between him and Eveleigh on the question. And it must not be forgotten that he paid Hooker his £20 nevertheless.

It may seem very probable that when, on 18 January 1598, the Company of Stationers concluded their deliberations upon the remedying of the excessive prices of books, it was no mere coincidence that this took place when it did. Book v of the *Ecclesiastical Polity* was published at the end of December 1597. The conversations of Hooker's stationer-friends with him were concurrent with discussions in the Hall of the Company, who were also considering at the same time another question closely related to the same publication, as we shall see.

The price settled by the Company for a book of the nature of the *Polity* was decided at the rate of two sheets per penny. The price finally fixed for Book v with its 72 sheets was therefore actually at the rate recommended. It might well seem that the stationers who saw Hooker were already aware what the recommendation was to be. Even the 1593 volume of Books i–iv with its 53 sheets was little above this rate— 2s. 6d. instead of 2s. 2½d. There was, quite clearly, no justification for the statement that the books had been priced too high, or that Sandys had sought to make an excessive profit in this way. Some memory may have persisted in Hooker's family of the debate upon the price of Book v. Hooker may well have talked upon the matter at home, reporting with pleasure upon his success in getting the price reduced by sixpence. Robert Churchman, for example, was positively insistent upon the view that Sandys had been too greedy in his demands when fixing prices for the books, thus damaging their sale. But the evidence of the booksellers concerned is definite, and does not support this view.

Did Sandys in fact stand to gain or to lose on his venture? His printing costs on the two volumes of 1593 and 1597 amounted to a total of £237. 10s. 0d., as we have calculated. The maximum receipts which could return to him from the complete sale of the whole edition at the price fixed would amount to £330. It certainly appears from Bill's evidence that he had to account to Sandys for the books at the rate of 2s. 6d. and 3s. respectively, whatever price he himself may have got for the book from the purchaser in his shop. This clearly meant that the books could never be sold to the purchaser at these minimum prices; the bookseller had to have his profit. It is difficult to believe that while Windet was the principal selling-agent he did not also have his profit on sales. He had certainly charged moderately for the printing. We may take it as fairly certain that the actual minimum retail prices were generally 3s. for the 1593 volume, 3s. 6d. for the 1597 volume, and 6s. 6d. for the two.

Sandys, it would seem, had left himself a fairly generous margin, with a possible profit of £92. 10s. 0d. But to recoup his expenditure on Books I–IV he had to sell 805 copies out of 1200, and on Book V the margin was smaller, 912 out of 1200. That is, he had to sell two-thirds of the first volume, and three-quarters of the second, before he saw his money back. It may seem that such a prospect was not one of undiluted pleasure in a publishing venture. Such apprehensions as he might justly have felt would, moreover, have been nourished by expert professional opinion. For the professional publishers had refused to undertake the risk, and had expressed not only their fears of financial failure but also their grounds for such fears, based on recent experience. In fact, if Sandys were thought of as a mere commercial venturer into the publishing trade, one would conclude that his optimism verged on foolhardiness.

Printers and publishers, however, are not immune from miscalculations. Their judgments are sometimes surprised by the market. Were they in this instance, in fact, right or wrong in their rejection of this classic of English literature, which was also an epoch-making book, as an unpromising prospect? Did they miss a chance of a best-seller? Or did they escape a serious loss?

There is no lack of evidence on the matter. The stationers were right, and their premonitions justified. The witnesses in Chancery make this amply clear. Several questions are asked about the failure of the book to sell, and explanations are suggested, principally that it was Sandys' fault for killing its sale by setting too high a price upon it. Bill the bookseller knew that a considerable number of copies were left on Sandys' hands unsold as late as in 1613. It is clear that this referred in fact to the 1597 volume, not the 1593 volume, as we shall see from other evidence. When asked about this, Bill rejects emphatically one suggested explanation. It was not the quality or repute of the book itself that was to blame. Nor does he accept the view that it was the fault either of

Sandys the publisher or of any bookseller. He was not aware, in fact, that the bad market for the *Ecclesiastical Polity*

grewe rather out of a desire of inordinate gaine by the Copies in Sandys or in any other whoe made proffit of the Copies vnder Sandys then out of any dislike taken out of the worke, neyther did I ever knowe or heare that the worke it self was ever disliked of any man of sound judgement, but allwaies holden and accompted a worke very famous and praiseworthie.

Bill, of course, was interested to uphold the probity of the booksellers, for he was one of those who 'made profit under' Sandys. We may set Bill's view, at any rate, against that of Robert Churchman, and against the protest of the stationers and Hooker's intervention to reduce the price of Book v. I am afraid that the conclusion must be simpler. The book was not in fact at the time a good commercial proposition, and the London publishers knew their business. The reasons they gave for holding off were the true reasons for the failure of the book to sell satisfactorily.

Bill states definitely that

the printed Copyes of the Bookes were in selling abowte thirtene yeres.

If we can take this to refer to both volumes, we may conclude that the 1593 edition of the first four Books was not exhausted before 1606, and the 1597 edition of Book v before 1610, to the best of Bill's knowledge. And we know that Bill had to do with selling copies of both volumes, as he told the Court, adding that he had his copies from Sandys, not from Windet. Bill, moreover, sold copies to other booksellers, which would send the price up to the ultimate customer.

Bill told William Stansby in 1611 that Sandys still had many of the copies of the book unsold on his hands. This was known to all the Stationers' Company, to which Sandys had appealed to arrange for their sale to Stansby.

It seems to be well enough established that the book had

a bad sale, even if there is some debate about its causes. And there is the most absolute confirmation of this evidence from another source.

Bibliographical science, in fact, had it been applied to extant copies of the early editions of the book, could have told the whole story. And the story it tells is the story which emerges from the evidence in Chancery, with modifications in detail. It is a striking vindication of methods of bibliographical analysis.

In the first place, it is clear that the 1593 volume of Books I–IV had not been sold out when the 1597 volume appeared. Arrangements were made for fixing a price for the two volumes to be sold together. All but one copy of the book known to me contain both volumes bound together. (I know no copy of Book V separately.) And in every instance the first parts are typographically and in every way undistinguishable by the closest analysis. It was quite unthinkable that the type should have been kept standing for four years or even less for a subsequent second impression; no Elizabethan press could have stood this; and it was contrary to regulation and practice to do so. If more copies had been needed, there would have been a new edition, and this would have been traceable from bibliographical examination.

Secondly, when we examine the 1604 edition, printed by Windet and containing Books I–V, we find that the new title-page justifies itself in respect of Books I–IV. For it is clear that here we have a new edition in every sense of the word. Books I–IV were set up afresh for this volume. By 1604, therefore, the 1200 copies of Books I–IV had been sold off, and there was a demand for more. Bill's recollection was only two years out. But the 1604 volume was not a new edition in respect of Book V. The bibliographical indications are conclusive. The sheets of Book V in the 1604 'edition' are identical with those of 1597. The volume, in fact, is a made-up book, containing new sheets of Books I–IV and old sheets of 1597. The 1200 copies of the 1597 volume had not been sold off by 1604. It seems clear that it was easier to sell the whole work, Books I–V, than either part separately, as indeed one would expect as soon as the second instalment was in print. The 1604 edition was, then, in part at least an attempt to sell off a considerable number of remainder sets of 1597 sheets, and money was invested to that intent in the reprint of Books I–IV.

This is exactly what one would have expected to find in any bibliographical enquiry, considering the evidence given in Chancery. And it is there to be found.

But who paid for this second edition of Books I–IV? Was it Sandys, and was it his idea to invest more money in his venture in order to obtain a more adequate return for that already invested? He was in London at the time, still a member of Parliament. There is no certain answer to this question, but I think it most likely that it was he, on the whole.

The next step, we might anticipate, would be a subsequent edition which would be determined by the need to sell off surplus copies of the second edition of Books I–IV, when all sets of the 1597 sheets of Book V had been disposed of with the help of part of that edition. The 1597 edition, Bill indicated, was sold off by about 1610. We might therefore expect a new volume, with a title-page about 1610, containing 1604 sheets of Books I–IV with new sheets of Book V. There is, in fact, an edition dated 1611, and we might reasonably start looking for 1611 jam to go with 1604 bread, just as we found 1604 jam to go with 1597 bread.

But the 1611 edition is a genuine new edition in all its parts. The situation, however, had completely changed. Windet was dead. And the new edition was set forth by William Stansby, his successor. And once more the evidence given in Chancery is in entire accordance with this phenomenon.

The clue to the changed situation is to be found in the

records of the Court of the Stationers' Company. Shortly after the publication of Book v of the *Ecclesiastical Polity*, the Court went into the question of the prices of books, and at the same time they discussed the growing practice of entering books for printing to stationers which were in fact being printed for outsiders, but entered as if they were the property of the stationer entering them. It was forbidden, on 19 January 1598, for any stationer henceforth to print any book unless the copy was his own, and the sale was to be for his own benefit and effected by members of the Company only. No outsider might take part in the sale or in the profits. The penalty was to be that the stationer contravening this order should lose all title to the book, which might be disposed of or reprinted at the discretion of the Company. The coincidence of time and subject is marked, and we may take it as probable that the publication of Hooker's book late in December 1597 was the determining occasion of these discussions and decisions.

Windet himself had a previous conviction on his record. He had already erred in 1589, when he printed Dr Timothy Bright's *Abridgement of the Book of Martyrs*, as assign for Bright, whence arose incidentally a quarrel with Richard Day, the owner of the complete *Book of Martyrs*. He was, however, allowed to reissue the *Ecclesiastical Polity* in 1604 and to try to round off the transaction with Sandys. But in 1611 his successor Stansby, who had no personal interest in the objects of the book, and no family connection with Hooker or Sandys, took his full rights under the new rule, with the agreement of the Company. He therefore reprinted the book on his own behalf and for his own profit, as if the copy were his own property, and without any reference to Sandys or his contract with Windet, his predecessor. The old, unsold sheets of the 1604 edition were no concern of his. And he simply took possession of the book as a literary property.

John Bill did not approve of this. He went to talk to

Stansby about it. It was unfair to Sandys, he protested, who had not been consulted and who had many copies of the book derelict. Indeed, he added, it would be unfair to Hooker's children who might profit from future sales of the book. Stansby's edition would kill Sandys' edition. The real reason, Bill argued in Court, why Windet's and Sandys' edition was not sold out was Stansby's competitive edition. In fact, he asserted, Sandys had not sold a single copy of the book since Stansby's edition came on the market. Naturally enough, any prospective purchaser of the book would prefer to have the latest and consequently the best edition. Not all the advantage conferred upon the 1604 edition by Dr Spenser's Preface to it would affect this preference. We may recall a historic instance of a First Folio of Shakespeare being turned out to make room in a great library for the later Second Folio. In any case, Stansby contentedly adopted the Preface to recommend his own edition. And he gave it an imposing and attractive title-page, engraved by Hole, to add to the effect of Spenser's Preface. It is interesting to note that the prospect of the book, as a commercial proposition, appears to have improved by 1611, as compared with 1593. The earlier editions may have created a market, so that Stansby reaped where Sandys had sown.

Stansby was, of course, interrogated in Chancery upon the general question of the ownership of the copy and the profits from its publication. He was asked whether he knew that Sandys had an interest in the book, and denied any knowledge of any such matter. Surely, he said, the five Books of the *Ecclesiastical Polity* were printed by Windet for his own profit, as his own venture. And if it was not Windet's venture he could not imagine whose it could have been. He was confronted with the actual contract between his predecessor and Sandys. Looking upon it and examining it, he was of course compelled to admit that it was apparently a contract, and that what he saw at its foot was Windet's own signature. But this did not shake his view. Stansby must have known all about it, in fact. He was in Windet's printing-house at the time, and probably had a hand in the printing of the book. But never was witness more economical of the truth than Stansby. The extent of his caution may be estimated from his reference to the *Ecclesiastical Polity* as the book

wherof Mr Hoker had the name to be the author,

on which point he does not care to commit himself to any opinion. For the rest, the copy was his now; there was no doubt about that; and he was going to print it for himself, now that there seemed to be better chances of a good sale.

A despairing effort was made by Sandys, confronted with this piracy, to make a deal with him, which Bill described. Sandys, hearing that Stansby had the book at press, reprinting it, approached the Master and Wardens of the Company with the petition that they should arrange with Stansby to buy from him at a reasonable rate all the copies left unsold on his hands. But Stansby refused, and evidently the Company declined to interfere, as indeed was inevitable after their decision of 1598. In a way, it is a pity that Stansby did not accept some such offer from Sandys. But for his refusal, the 1611 edition would have offered a very pretty puzzle to the detective bibliographer. Some copies would have contained a reissue of the sheets of the earlier editions, and some would have contained a genuine reprint. As it is, we should expect to find his edition completely re-set throughout, a true new edition. And this is exactly what we find in fact.

If the bibliographer has been deprived of this pleasure by Stansby, another puzzle is presented by a later edition, which is even superior in its attractions as a puzzle. And the solution is pleasurably exciting. In a copy of one of Stansby's editions, in University College, London, we find preliminary matter dated 1632, followed to our surprise by sheets of Books I–IV belonging to Windet's edition of 1604. The remainder of the volume consists of 1632 material. It is easy to dismiss such books as 'made-up copies'. But this is no explanation, unless we know when and by whom the 'making-up' was done. It is an evasion of a problem. It is the less satisfactory when we know that there are other copies in the same state.[1]

These 1604 sheets are a mystery, incorporated in a 1632 volume, and apparently sold in this form by Stansby. If he had 1604 sheets of Books I–IV over, why did he reprint these Books in 1611, or why is there no copy of the 1611 edition with such sheets? We know that Stansby refused to purchase them from Sandys. The 1604 edition, printed by Windet, belonged to Sandys, and the sheets were his. Then how is it that after so many years Stansby had in his possession a stock of these sheets, and worked them off in this medley of 1632?

The answer is surely to be found in a little story which Stansby could have told with a chuckle. Sandys could not dispose of his sheets to Stansby, or to anyone else. They were left derelict in Windet's shop. For Windet was certainly storing Sandys' sheets for him. Stansby bought up Windet's business in 1611 when Windet died, and continued in his shop. But he could not touch Sandys' sheets; they were not part of Windet's stock; so he left them there. Sandys rose in the world, high enough to become Treasurer of the Virginia Company by 1619; important enough for King James to acknowledge his eminence by putting him in the Tower for a few months in 1621. Sandys let his little publishing venture slip from his mind; it had indeed slipped through his fingers in 1611. Stansby bided his time. A true Autolycus, at the right moment he snapped up this uncon-sidered trifle of printed sheets, and turned them to account. For Sandys died in 1629, and next time Stansby went round his store-room, poking about, he came on this pile of sheets, with no one to claim them, his own at last. And the logical consequence is the existence of these copies of a 1632 edition of Hooker's *Ecclesiastical Polity*. So at long last Stansby

[1] Mr Tillotson informs me that there are two such copies at Oxford, one in the English Library and one at Corpus Christi, Hooker's College.

acceded to Sandys' request made in 1611 that he would take over his sheets and dispose of them, paying a reasonable price. The price was eminently reasonable—from Stansby's point of view. In fact, he must have mused pleasurably on the occasional solaces to a publisher's strenuous life.

If the *Ecclesiastical Polity* was a slow and difficult seller while it was Sandys' property, it was otherwise in the later history of the book. Sandys probably did little more than at best to balance his account upon the book. But Stansby seems to have found a good market for it, to judge by the frequent editions which appeared with his imprint. And he had paid nothing for his property in it. When he died, his successors continued to publish it at intervals, with the same apparent success. It is pleasing to observe that Stansby over-came his scepticism about the authorship of the book sufficiently to commit himself on his title-pages to the assertion that the *Ecclesiastical Polity* was 'By Richard Hooker'.

But it appears plainly enough that, if Hooker himself was rewarded for his immense labours to the extent of Sandys' payment of £30, his daughters were in no way benefited by the publication of the book.

Chapter III

THE POSTHUMOUS BOOKS OF
THE LAWS OF ECCLESIASTICAL POLITY

§i. THE LEGEND OF THE DESTRUCTION
OF HOOKER'S MANUSCRIPTS

Traditional authority and accepted opinion, it may seem, has offered but little resistance to the new facts and conclusions put forward so far, in respect of questions of importance in Hooker's lifetime. But Hooker's biographer, and the historian of his great work, is bound to consider no less closely the fate of the literary legacy he left behind him at his death. In particular, the fate of the manuscripts containing the last three Books of the *Ecclesiastical Polity*, Books VI–VIII, is of the highest significance to the bibliographer also and, it will appear, to the student of religious history no less.

Here, a strong body of more apparently authentic report supports the accepted version so well known, in one form, as contained in Walton's *Life*. Indeed, the new information now available furnishes yet more evidence pointing in the same direction. Yet the conclusion is bound to be the rejection of all views of the question hitherto advanced.

Hooker, it is known, died in 1600, having seen printed in his lifetime Books I–IV in 1593, and Book V in 1597. But it would seem that he wrote his work in eight Books. It is described as 'The Laws of Ecclesiastical Polity Eight Books' in the Stationers' Register and as licensed under that title by Archbishop Whitgift; and it is also so described on the title-page of the first edition. It has been argued from this by some that all eight Books were already written then, in 1593, and that the manuscript sent to Whitgift and, as it was

believed, to Burleigh, contained all eight. Some hold that
the remaining three Books, unpublished at the time of
Hooker's death, were written between 1597 and 1600, and
were left by him in manuscript, completed and ready for the
press. A third alternative is offered by Mr Houk, that the
three Books were completed by 1593, and subsequently
revised and made ready again by 1600.

Whatever the preliminary history of these completed
manuscripts, after Hooker's death their precious perfection
was interfered with by sinister persons, with the collusion of
his widow Joan. The fair copies were burned or destroyed,
leaving only fragmentary, rough drafts, so imperfect that it
was judged unfit to print them, and that it involved so much
work to set them in any kind of order that they could not
be published until some fifty years after. Books VI and VIII
were, in fact, first printed in the 1648 edition, and Book VII
not until Gauden's 1661 edition, the first to contain all the
eight Books which the title-page had been promising ever
since 1593.

The principal evidence for the completion of all eight
Books by Hooker before his death is the definite statement
of William Covel in 1603, only three years after Hooker's
death, when he printed a defence of Hooker's five Books
against a printed attack upon them, the *Christian Letter* of
1599. Covel's words bear all the apparent authority of
immediate and first-hand information, as from Hooker's
own affirmation:

> Concerning those three Books of his, which from his own
> mouth I am informed that they were finished, I know not in
> whose hands they are.

To go against such a statement, it would seem, we should
have to convict either Hooker or Covel of untruth, or Covel
of a misapprehension. But we are not, in fact, driven to this.
Covel's exact words do not conveniently bear the meaning
that he himself heard this statement made by Hooker or that

Hooker himself gave him this information. The phrase used, 'I *am* informed', suggests recent information from a third person, information at second hand. Had Covel used the phrase 'I *was* informed', the words would have borne a very different sense, and they would have weighed very heavily indeed in the balance.

There is greater difficulty, perhaps, in disposing of the observation made by Dr Spenser, also in print, in the Preface he contributed to the 1604 edition of the *Polity*, to the effect that Hooker 'lived till he saw them perfected'. His statement, made on his own authority, must be left for the moment.

With this evidence is very closely associated the evidence bearing upon the destruction of the manuscripts of the last three Books. First comes a letter from Bishop Andrewes, of which only a copy has survived in a Commonplace Book, and apparently written to Dr Parry immediately on hearing the news of Hooker's death. In this letter warning is given that care should be taken to ensure the safety of the manuscripts, lest they be 'embezelled' and so suppressed, or come 'into great hands' who will mutilate them for their own purposes. Once more, the precise wording of the letter is highly significant. It should be observed, moreover, that Andrewes bids Dr Parry (to whom this letter was certainly written) get into touch with Joan Hooker or with John Churchman for that purpose, hoping that the manuscripts may come into the custody, not of great persons, but of

some of them that unfeinedly wish'd him well, though of the meaner sort.

The words might well be taken, not to exclude Joan or Churchman from the category of desirable custodians, but almost to specify them. The rest of Andrewes' letter, indeed, bears out the suggestion that he took a very favourable view of Churchman, as a well-wisher to Hooker and his work. But there is no doubt that the Bishop was openly apprehensive about the possible fate of the manuscripts.

Next in date comes Dr Spenser's story of the actual outrage
upon the manuscripts. It is told in his Preface to the 1604
edition, after he has mentioned the tentative proposals for
printing the last three Books:

> But some evill disposed mindes, whether of malice, or covetous-
> nesse, or wicked blind Zeale, it is uncerteine,...as soone as they
> were borne, and their father dead, smothered them, and by
> conveying away the perfect Copies, left unto us nothing but
> certaine olde unperfect and mangled draughts, dismembered into
> peeces, and scattered like Medeas Absyrtus.

The main legend in subsequent writers is obviously derived
from Spenser. Gauden's *Life* repeats it, using the exact word
'smother'. And it is clear that Walton's informant, to whom
he owed his elaborate story of Mr Chark's visit to Hooker's
study, the tearing and burning of the papers, of Mrs Hooker's
examination by the Privy Council, her confession and her
death next morning, was the same informant whom he
quotes later in his Appendix. It was his aunt, sister to George
Cranmer, and wife to Dr Spenser. As for Bishop King's
Letter, attached to Walton's *Life*, his informant was his father,
who in turn derived his knowledge from 'the learned
Dr John Spencer'. I have no doubt whatever that Covel's
informant also was Dr Spenser.

Spenser, it is true, is a witness not lightly to be put aside.
He was President of Corpus Christi College, Hooker's own
College, and a man of high repute. But it is well to realize
in the first place that in all probability we have only the one
authority responsible for all the mass of statements repeated
at various times from 1603 to 1665 and subsequently.

A new and detailed statement on the question may now
be added to the many already extant, which may at first sight
appear to confirm them. In the course of the Chancery
proceedings, when enquiry was made into the whole problem of the manuscripts left behind by Hooker, with a view
to proving that his daughters had not had their fair profit

from their father's literary work, a very interesting deposition was made on the particular point now under discussion. The witness who testified was Edmund Parbo, a London lawyer, of Staple Inn, forty-three years of age on the day on which he gave evidence, on 3 June 1614. Parbo appears to be actually the only independent authority on this matter except Dr Spenser, and he has a circumstantial story to tell:

after the deceasse of Mr Hooker...one Nethersole did marry with his wyddowe by meanes whereof dyvers of the bookes and written woorks of...Mr Hooker came to the hands of him...Nethersole And (as this deponent hath Credibly heard and verely beleeveth it to be true)...Nethersole one Mr Raven the Schoole master of Canterbury and one Mr Aldridge Combyning themselves together did labor to subpresse the written bookes & woorks of... Mr Richard Hooker, and (as this deponent hath likewise heard,) the better to effect their purpose they...Nethersole Raven and Aldridge did burne or cause to be burned all or most of the written woorks of...Mr Rychard Hooker which soe came to their hands.

Could any story appear to be more authentic? We know about Nethersole and his marriage with Joan Hooker. I find that there were Aldridges who were Churchman's, and formerly Hooker's, neighbours in St Augustine's in London. Yet we cannot fail to observe that Parbo's details clash with such details as we have elsewhere. Instead of Mrs Hooker, Chark and an unnamed minister, we now have Nethersole, Raven the schoolmaster and Aldridge, and Canterbury instead of Bishopsbourne. Truly it might seem as if any dog were good enough to be beaten with this stick. We may recall that it was another schoolmaster of Canterbury, not Raven but Edward Turfett, who was involved as a fellow-conspirator with Nethersole and the Pettifers in their forgery of a deed, and in their ordeal in Star Chamber.

Parbo replied to the usual enquiry in Court that he knew personally Sandys, Hooker, and Churchman, but that he did not know Hooker's daughters. One may wonder therefore how he could possibly know of his own knowledge what happened at Canterbury upon Joan's remarriage, for the daughters were living there at the time. The fact is, of course, that it is all hearsay again, and Parbo himself makes this quite clear. Once more, it is second-hand evidence after all. And a little dust of research is stirred by this fresh pother. Nethersole, it is true, might be judged to be capable of anything to annoy. But Roger Raven, Headmaster of the King's School at Canterbury from 1591 to 1615, and formerly Master of Wrotham School in Kent, was actually Archbishop Whitgift's nominee, pressed by him upon the Dean and Chapter of Canterbury.[1] 'One Mr Aldridge' was obviously Dr Francis Aldrich, Master of Sidney Sussex College in Cambridge, and a friend of Raven's. They were both Clare Hall men, and Raven was the overseer appointed by Aldrich's will, in 1609. Aldrich's interests and turn of mind may well be thought to be reflected in his particular disposal of his editions of Aquinas, Zanchius and Bernard, the last of these being left to Raven. It would be difficult to choose more unlikely candidates for the office of Puritan destroyers of the work of the apologist for the Church of England. Aldrich was buried in St Margaret's Church in Canterbury. But there is no support for Parbo's slander, four years after his death, that he had been a traitor to the cause upon which the foundations of Canterbury rested, and that Geneva was his spiritual home. Parbo's deposition may surely be dismissed.

Why, we may well ask, was the question not put directly in Court to John or Robert Churchman, to Eveleigh, or to Spenser himself? Spenser, it is true, referred obliquely to the matter when he gave evidence in 1613, commenting upon the manuscripts that he helped to examine, and his remark is of interest. It is in the form of a parenthesis

[1] Canon John Shirley, Headmaster of the King's School, kindly gave me information about his predecessor Raven. See Appendix C, III.

(the Choyce writings of...Mr Hooker which were most desyred being kept away from this deponent and the rest or vtterly perished)

and suggests two different possibilities, both varying from his 1604 statement and from other rival versions. It is a fact of significance that the specific question was put only to Parbo, and was not put to Spenser, though it was of considerable value to Sandys' defence to have strong evidence on the point. Was Parbo the only witness prepared to commit himself? Did Spenser boggle at giving evidence upon it? Knowing the ways of legal matters at the time, we may fairly conclude that this is the true explanation. It is well to remember that Spenser was quite definitely on Sandys' side. He was one of Sandys' intimates. Sandys was a Corpus man, a former Fellow of Spenser's College, and Spenser's loyalty might fairly be bound rather to the living than to the daughters of the dead, especially where their cause was suspect in the eyes of Sandys, Cranmer's family, and probably of the whole community of Corpus.

Spenser might well have hesitated if asked to answer directly. The question was put to him, however, in another form. His reply gives yet another variant to the story, and this time it is surely the first and original variant that underlies the rest. Sandys, Spenser said,

cominge to heare that it was supposed that the perfect coppies of those 3 latter books were concealed in regard that he the... defendant was to have the proffitt of the printinge of them he... affirmed in this deponents hearinge that soe as hee might be a saver in regarde of the charges that he had beene formerly at about the other books, that he for his parte would be well contented that the now complainants shoulde have the benefitt of those three latter bookes.

This may perhaps be interpreted in two ways. Either Sandys meant that he would be ready to cut his losses by abandoning his claim to the copy of Books VI–VIII. He would then incur no further capital costs by financing their printing or by paying Hooker's estate the sum of £20 unpaid out of the total of·£50 promised for the whole work. Or he meant that he would be content to abandon his claims provided that he was repaid his losses on the financing of Books I–V, whether by continued belated sales or otherwise. I am inclined to think the latter interpretation is the more probable. 'To save', in Elizabethan English, often means 'to recover'.

Spenser agrees that he himself had related this to Huntley when endeavouring to intervene in the case with a view to a friendly compromise. Certainly it seems that Spenser is hard put to it to decide between 'Malice or covetousnesse, or wicked blind Zeale', in his varying accounts of the matter. And whatever version of the tale he accepts for the time being, he has nothing but rumour to go upon. Like Sandys, he merely 'came to hear that it was supposed'. There is no sort of indication that Spenser could have been at or near Bishopsbourne at the time of Hooker's death or immediately after. He was then the incumbent of St Sepulchre's in London, and was in touch only with the Londoners connected with Hooker and his family. Nor was his wife, the original source of these stories, in any better case to know.

Parbo certainly was a Kentish man, as we learn from the record of Lincoln's Inn, to which he was admitted in 1619. But Sandwich is not Canterbury or Bishopsbourne. And he is careful to say that he is speaking at second-hand. The Cranmers were a great Canterbury family, ascending through the Registrar to the Archdeacon and the Archbishop. George Cranmer was in Ireland on the day of Hooker's death, and was himself killed a few days later. Spenser's wife was George's sister, and there can be no reasonable doubt that he had his information from her and from her brother William, as did Sandys, and Walton many years after. Once more, we return to a Cranmer source as authority. And we have seen how untrustworthy this source was upon other matters, and how deeply prejudiced against Hooker's wife and her family.

There is, in fact, no first-hand evidence for any foundation for the story as a whole concerning the completion and the destruction of the copy for the last three Books of the *Polity*. The story, in its various forms, presents some impossibilities. Mrs Hooker's impeachment, her journey to London, her examination before the Privy Council, and her death, are manifest myth. And the various versions are mutually destructive by their many incompatibilities.

We cannot fail to observe that all these versions, agreeing in one respect only, depend for even plausibility upon the representation of Mrs Hooker and her family as willing to be accessories to the destruction or the concealment of the last three Books of the *Polity*, and in general upon the conception of Hooker's relations with the Churchmen which have now been shown to be gravely distorted by Walton along with other historians. The parallel suggestion that Mrs Hooker and her father were of the Puritan party, and therefore might have connived at suppressing the three Books, is also a patent absurdity now, in the light of the true story of those relations. The precise words of Lancelot Andrewes have not been sufficiently attended to. Yet they are highly significant. He fears the intervention of 'great hands', not of Hooker's family, in whom he rests his confidence, nor of local wreckers. He apprehends the activities of men in high position, concerned in the great controversy on the opposite side to Hooker and to himself, or at any rate in a different wing of the movement.

A final suggestion may be added as in some measure a relief from the necessity of attributing irresponsible distortions of truth, amounting to invention, to the Cranmer family. The legend may conceivably have arisen in part out of an incident that Walton mentions in his *Life*, and that may well deserve to be taken into account in this connection. During Hooker's last illness, shortly before his death, Walton tells us how Hooker's house was entered by robbers who, however, to his great relief, did not touch his papers. It is quite possible that upon such a basis of fact should have been evolved the elaborate story, with all its variants, that has been recorded. Romance, epic, legend, saga, nay history also, offer abundant parallels to such creative confusions in the passing of story from mouth to mouth, especially with prejudice to be served in the process. It was an age of ill-natured, irresponsible and reckless gossip, as well as of splendours of courage, generosity and benevolence. The Blatant Beast was abroad in the land of the Faerie Queen of England, and Edmund Spenser knew better than to imagine even a fictitious end to its evil work.

There is also, of course, a major premise upon which any such legend must be rested, namely that Hooker had in fact completed the writing of the last three Books of the *Polity*, and that fair copies of these Books were among his papers at Bishopsbourne. The suggestion deserves closer consideration. There appears to be no trustworthy evidence at first hand that the Books were completed. Certainly what evidence there is needs to be confirmed before we can accept it. But what facts we possess seem definitely to tell against acceptance.

First, we should consider the question of the time available for composition of the *Polity*. By the end of 1592 Hooker had, as we know, drawn up the complete plan for the whole work in eight Books, and sketched it in outline. He had also written the first four Books and had them copied out fair, ready for the press. There is every reason for rejecting the theory that he had completed the writing of all eight Books by then, that they were all contained in the copy sent to Whitgift, all read and licensed by him, all presented and registered in the Stationers' Hall, and then published piecemeal after delay and subsequent revision due mainly to the need for obtaining Burleigh's approval and to meet his criticisms. Such a view, as maintained by Mr Houk for instance, hangs on the mere form of words of the title-page and entry in the Stationers' Register, and on misinterpretation of Hooker's letter to Burleigh. The form of words is Hooker's, and was inevitable.

It was clearly the intention of Hooker and of his publishers —and incidentally of Sandys—that the book should be brought out in instalments and ultimately bound together. The volumes of 1593, of 1597, and of 1604 were all uniform in print and format, deliberately for that purpose. Hooker's 'Advertisement to the Reader', appended to the 1593 edition of Books I–IV, announces this decision and this policy:

> I Have for some causes (gentle Reader) thought it at this time more fit to let goe these foure bookes by themselues, then to stay both them and the rest, till the whole might together be published.

The 'causes' he refers to here need consideration. And he points out that these four Books form a unit, covering the main general positions upon which his book as a whole is founded, and upon which the Church of England rested its case. Let us also remember the great persons who in the Chancery suit are referred to as 'hastening' his book. And then let us consider the actual date of publication, now established, coinciding with the opening of the debate upon Nonconformity in Parliament in March 1593, in which Sandys was a prominent figure.

The whole work was planned; the title-page promised the whole work in due course; for the present the plan and the first four Books were printed; and Hooker explained the situation to those who purchased this instalment, as he did again on the publication of Book V in 1597. When he then published this second instalment of his promised undertaking, his words are even more unmistakable in their significance:

> To the Reader. Have patience with me for a small time, and by the help of Almightie God I will pay the whole.

Are these the words of a man concerned with problems of publishing delays or other technical difficulties? Or are they not rather those of a man struggling with an enormous task and burden laid upon him, which he is labouring to complete? It may seem that the help of divine power might more fitly be invoked by Hooker for the writing of this book in God's service. There was no impediment now to the printing and publishing of the rest of the book. Sandys' help, with Windet's collaboration, was sufficient to this end, for which divine intervention was not required. But Hooker's share of the task was too much for him, in the time at his disposal before his untimely death. We may well feel some tragic quality in Hooker's words here, some reflection of his sense of the burden of his task and of his promise. He never 'paid the whole'.

If further confirmation is desired, we need only to turn to the extant manuscript of Book v, which bears the autograph signature and licence of Archbishop Whitgift. Why did this section of the work need his separate licence, if the whole eight Books had already been approved and licensed by him? Surely the fact is that Book v was written subsequently to the licensing and printing of Books i–iv and, when finished, was submitted to the Archbishop as a necessary preliminary to its publication. There was no need for any further entry in the Stationers' Register.

Let us, again, consider the time-factor. There is some evidence that the work began to be seriously considered about 1588, when Hooker and Sandys were first resident together in Churchman's house, when Sandys first entered Parliament, and when the problem of Puritan nonconformity was seen to be definitely more critical than that of Catholic recusancy, after the defeat of the Armada. For the *Polity* is aimed against Geneva, not against Rome. Four to five years is a reasonable allowance for the vast reading, study and discussion that must have gone to the formulation of the general plan of the book as a whole, together with the actual writing of the first four Books upon Generalities. Nearly five years pass before Book v is completed, in length greater than the previous four Books together. Three years only remain of Hooker's life, from the printing of Book v in December 1597 to his death in November 1600, for the completion of three more Books, one of which deals with the most critical, the most contentious, and the thorniest of all his problems, that of the royal supremacy in ecclesiastical matters. Nor were the other two Books by any means plain sailing, as will appear. We have the extant record of searching examination by Sandys and Cranmer of Hooker's draft for one of them. And this was the next in order, Book VI.

It was to the interest of all parties concerned that the work should be completed and set forth as a whole, and it was clearly the intention that the publication of Books I–IV should be followed up as soon as possible by the rest of the *Polity*. Whitgift did not stand in the way. Nor could Burleigh. The printing was arranged for under contract. But Hooker could not redeem his promise. Nor need we wonder at this, when we realize his conception of his duty to his vast theme. If it is evident that the whole work could not conceivably have been completed by the end of 1592, it is no less evident that the writing of Books VI–VIII could not have been begun and finished between 1597 and 1600, in the intervals of the duties of a clergyman in charge of a parish.

The evidence from Chancery so far supports this view of the matter. Sandys had paid Hooker £10 for the manuscript of Books I–IV. He had subsequently paid him £20 on receipt of the manuscript of Book v, and held up the remaining £20 promised, pending the completion of the work. And the further evidence given on the question of Hooker's manuscripts sets out facts that bear out these conclusions, and are, incidentally, of considerable interest in other ways.

§ ii. THE TREASURE FROM BISHOPSBOURNE

When the news of Hooker's death reached John Churchman
in London, Hooker's father-in-law and overseer of his will,
Churchman at once took steps to fulfil his duties. He sent
a trusted and competent employee of his own to Bishopsbourne—it is Philip Culme himself from whom we know
this—to Hooker's house, to make an inventory of his books
and to attend immediately to the question of his manuscripts.
It is evident that this was a matter of importance in Churchman's mind, and that there was no delay in taking action.
Culme's orders were to make search in Hooker's house and
in his study for all manuscripts to be found there, whether in
book-form or in stray papers. Having collected all he could
find, he was to bring them all back with him to London to
Churchman's house. He carried out his instructions. It is
evident that the total quantity of manuscript was considerable,
enough to fill a cloak-bag, the Elizabethan equivalent of a
portmanteau. It was, said Churchman, a 'reasonable big'
cloak-bag, and it was filled with the papers collected by
Culme. It was not Culme's business to make an inventory
of the papers, but merely to take charge of them at once, to
prevent any negligent handling or any interference with
them, and to get them as soon as possible into safe keeping.
There is no manner of hint of any impediment put in the
way of this safeguarding of the precious manuscripts on the
part of Mrs Hooker or of anyone else.

So John Churchman seems to have met the wishes of
Lancelot Andrewes and to have seen that this important duty
was fulfilled exactly as Andrewes hoped, to the exclusion of
any possibility of interference with Hooker's papers by any
of the feared 'great hands'. The next step was to see that
they were entrusted to the proper hands for further disposal
with a view to publication. Churchman, no doubt, consulted Sandys in the matter. Sandys was obviously deeply
interested in the manuscripts bearing upon the last three

Books of the *Polity*. Dr John Spenser was a trustee under Hooker's will and a notable divine, subsequently a chaplain to King James and one of the authors of the great Bible, obviously a proper person in all respects. Finally they added to their number Dr Parry, subsequently Bishop of Worcester.

There was some inevitable delay. But before a year had passed after Hooker's death, these three men were collected together at Churchman's house. Being so gathered in conclave, Churchman handed over to them the cloak-bag with its contents which had been brought up from Bishopsbourne. They opened it and proceeded to the examination of the remaining treasure of Hooker's mind. It must have been a moment of memorable import. For it is clear that none of those gathered round Churchman's table, not even Churchman or Sandys, knew what was to be expected. So paper after paper was brought forth from the bag and laid out upon the table before the expert eyes of the committee, which proceeded to their analysis and inventory. Dr Spenser gives the fullest and most detailed account of the contents of the treasure-bag.

There were two piles of manuscript, easily recognized as being the sixth and seventh Books of the *Polity*, apparently in some completeness though not in finished shape. A third pile belonged obviously to the eighth Book, but consisted only of separate sections and scattered fragments or sketches with no coherence or sequence, *disjecta membra* of the Book. There were also miscellaneous manuscripts having no connection with the *Polity*. There were, for example, the complete copies of some sermons preached by Hooker. Also manuscripts containing drafts and notes for various discourses, and among them the incomplete copy for an answer to a book written against Hooker, doubtless for Hooker's answer to the *Christian Letter* of 1599. The treasure was thus considerable, both in respect of further material for the *Polity* and of Hooker's minor works.

At this meeting, the committee went no further than to

make this general analysis and inventory of the chief heads under which the manuscript papers seemed to fall, for there was a good deal of confusion and disorder in the material. They therefore, after this preliminary survey, handed the whole *corpus* of writings over to Sandys to sort them all out under their proper heads. Sandys took them away home with him to get on with this task, and in due course brought them back to Churchman's house for a second meeting of the committee, now arranged in such order as was possible. It would appear that Lancelot Andrewes had by now been added to the committee, though he did not attend the meeting.

The material was now divided up for distribution between Spenser, Parry and Andrewes, evidently with the consent of Churchman and of Mrs Hooker. The Doctors were prepared to undertake the task of working over the manuscripts with a view to preparing them for the press. All that bore upon the last three Books of the *Polity* were handed over to Spenser, while the sermons and other minor works were allocated to Parry and Andrewes between them for their editorial labours. It is certain that Spenser carried out his duty and his undertaking. But it is less clear that Parry and Andrewes completed their task. Part at least of the material allocated to them, in particular the sermons, was soon back in Sandys' possession, if indeed it ever left him, as we shall see.

According to Dr Spenser two important sections of Hooker's posthumous work were in such an advanced state that they could readily be prepared for the press. Hooker's drafts of Books VI and VII of the *Polity*, and a small collection of sermons, needed only 'reasonable travail and pains' on the part of their editors to be made fit for printing. It was true that when so printed they would be far from the finished and perfected product that Hooker would have made of them according to his own intentions. But even so the imperfect material was well worth printing, and Hooker's friends fully intended to set about its publication. To this end they proposed to put into order his drafts of the two Books of the *Polity*, setting them in shape as well as possible without alteration or addition. As for the important eighth Book, they gave close consideration to the possibility of making what they could out of the mass of disjointed fragments and sections which had come to them out of the cloak-bag in Hooker's rough drafts.

Spenser himself completed one part of his labour upon his friend's posthumous work. He did all that could be done with the manuscripts of the sixth and seventh Books, and brought them 'to some reasonable perfection'. So when he contributed an address 'To the Reader', prefixed to the 1604 edition of Books I–V of the *Polity*, he announced the intention to complete the printing of the whole work by publishing Books VI–VIII, in however truncated a form. 'There is a purpose of setting forth', he wrote, 'the three last Books also, their Fathers Posthumi.' And after relating the story of Hooker's completion of his work and of the loss of 'the perfect Copies', he cites the insistence of persons of importance as reason for the proposal to publish even Hooker's 'old unperfect and mangled Draughts', though if Hooker had lived to see them in print in this form he might well have 'named them *Benonies*, the Sons of Sorrow'. All that can be hoped for is that they should show 'some shadows and resemblances of their Fathers face'.

The important fact here is that it had been definitely agreed and concluded that these last Books should be published, after editorial preparation. The imperfect state of the work was not to stand in the way of their publication. What Spenser wrote in his Preface of 1604 is confirmed in his evidence in Chancery nine years later. And the editorial work in respect of Books VI and VII was completed by Spenser; he had brought them, he said in 1613, 'to some reasonable perfection'.

§ iii. THE SUPPRESSION OF HOOKER'S POSTHUMOUS MANUSCRIPTS

There was one further possible impediment to the publication of this material, either in whole or in part, which has not been taken into account. Hooker's posthumous manuscripts and papers were, after all, part of his estate. They had not been bequeathed by him to any legatee. They therefore fell into the residuary estate to which Mrs Hooker was entitled. Did she, or her family, intervene to prevent or delay publication? Upon this question there can be no conceivable doubt. It is agreed on all sides—indeed it is part of Sandys' case that this was so—that the manuscripts were committed to Sandys, Spenser, Parry and Andrewes 'to be disposed by their common consent, as they should think fittest', by Mrs Hooker and by John Churchman. It was entirely to the interest of the family that the material should be printed, both for the honour of their father and in the hope of financial benefit. It is well to remember that the question that gave birth to all this valuable evidence upon the history of Hooker's literary work was the question whether Hooker's daughters had been deprived of the profits due to them from the publishing of that work, both the earlier printed Books and the posthumous later Books and papers. As to this latter part of the question, Spenser only remarked that he could not say whether, if printed, they would have proved to be saleable or profitable. But it is clear that Mrs Hooker herself, who owned the manuscripts; Churchman, to whom she sent them in trust; and Sandys and the Doctors, to whom their fate was committed; all had the best intentions.

As early as in 1604, in his Preface to the edition of that year, Spenser had announced 'a purpose of setting forth the last three Books'. In 1613 he declared that at some unspecified time ago he had completed the editorial work which had brought Books VI and VII 'to some reasonable perfection'.

Upon all these facts we could confidently have anticipated an edition of the *Polity*, which should have included at least these two Books, at some time prior to the edition of 1611, or at least an edition of these two Books alone.

There were, of course, complications by late in 1611, when Stansby succeeded to Windet and jumped Sandys' claim to the copyright in the *Polity*. In general, Stansby's piratical action queered the pitch for any further publishing venture by Sandys in relation to the *Polity* after 1611. But Windet did not transfer his copyrights to Stansby until towards the end of the year, in September 1611, and was still master of his printing-house until then, and presumably still of the same mind towards Hooker and Sandys. It is evident enough that there was a market for the *Polity* in 1611, or Stansby would not have ventured upon his edition with its elaborate title-page, at his own cost. And surely an edition which for the first time was enlarged by the inclusion of the hitherto unprinted Books VI and VII would have had an even better market. It would surely also have offered to Sandys a better hope of working off his unsold sheets than his subsequent vain approach to Stansby to take them off his hands. The interdict laid by the Stationers' Company upon publishing on commission, in 1597, had clearly not been enforced rigidly. The 1604 edition is the proof of this in respect of Sandys' transactions with Windet. Certainly we could not have anticipated to find in Stansby's 1611 edition the new Books prepared for the press by Spenser. But on all counts we might have expected a new edition before 1611, printed by Windet for Sandys, of *The Laws of Ecclesiastical Polity*, Books I–VII. Such an edition did not, in fact, ever appear. The copy for the last three Books of the *Polity*, which came into the hands of Sandys and his fellows in 1600 or 1601 at latest, lay concealed and sterile for almost fifty years. Not until 1648 did any part of this material find its way into print, when Bishop's edition included Books VI and VIII. Book VII was still suppressed, and did not appear until

Gauden printed it in his edition of 1661, when for the first time the original title-page of 1593, promising the reader eight Books of *The Laws of Ecclesiastical Polity*, was justified. We may well wonder what caused this inordinate and incomprehensible delay in printing the last three Books of the *Polity*, and in particular, in the light of these facts, of Books VI and VII. It is difficult not to suspect some deliberate suppression of the material left by Hooker, where no other factor, or combination of factors, appears to satisfy the enquiring mind.

Some alleviations of the quandary may, it is true, be put forward. We might be content to suggest that the zeal of Sandys diminished as the years went by, with the passing of the immediate crisis in the affairs of the Church, and with his own increasing absorption in new interests, in the great part he was playing in colonial affairs and in political life. And doubtless this was one of the factors to be taken into account. The printer Windet may have been no less insistent than before upon a guarantee of the cost of printing, and Sandys disinclined to undertake further expense. He had been somewhat disillusioned by his experience of such publishing ventures, and may have thought above all of cutting his losses.

One could hardly hope for further enlightenment upon the question. Yet it is, in fact, illuminated by the proceedings in Chancery, and the new light thrown upon the difficulty is disturbing. We may well recall here the intuitive qualms felt by the nonconformist Coleridge, who was convinced that the High Church party disliked part of the contents of the last three Books and therefore cast doubts on their authenticity.[1] And we may recall also Lancelot Andrewes' fears for the safety of Hooker's manuscripts at the hands of persons of high estate. Suspicions of this nature are bound to shake the ground beneath our feet in considering the ramifications of the arguments for the position of the Church of

---

[1] *Literary Remains* (1838), III, pp. 19–20. Hallam had offered a similar suggestion in 1827. See Appendix D, III.

England in the seventeenth century. When the main battle was won, as it was won when the sixteenth century came to its close, there was scope for increasing diversity of opinion and for the hardening of those divergences into opposing schools of thought. Upon the Church of England, standing in a measure midway between the authoritarian Catholic position and that of the Puritan dissenters, there broke tides of thought from both quarters the impulse of which became manifest in the history of this living institution. Hooker could at best, though he could lay the firm foundations on which the Church rested, seize its general position for a moment, or a decade, in its history.

Dr Spenser, after narrating what he knew of the history of Hooker's manuscripts and of his own share in their disposal, went on to inform the Court that, though he himself had completed the editing of Books VI and VII, they were 'not yet thought fitt for the press', and adds that he is not prepared to state the reason for this decision, if the Court will permit him to remain silent upon this point. It is obviously no question of the form of the material; Spenser himself has certified us upon this; it is some question of the matter contained in it. Fortunately the question put to Spenser is still extant, and gives us the requisite information. Spenser does not deny the suggestions in the question; he is content to evade the issue by a refusal to answer.

About August 1611 Spenser conferred with Huntley and with Robert Churchman, with a view to a friendly settlement of all matters outstanding between Hooker's daughters and Sandys and to averting legal proceedings. And he then informed Huntley that some years earlier it had been fully intended to publish the last three Books of the *Polity*. But publication had been postponed because of a difference of opinion between Sandys and Lancelot Andrewes. They could not agree together about the admission into the publication of 'a tract of confession written by their father'. This is the suggestion of the interrogatory; it comes from

Huntley himself and arises out of an interview with Spenser; and Spenser does not deny it. We may fairly take it as authentic evidence of fact. So it seems that the printing of the last three Books, or part of them, was prevented by a difference of opinion between Sandys and Andrewes some years before 1611, and that the impediment was a matter of doctrinal rather than of editorial policy.

There is no mistaking the probable line of division existing between Sandys and Andrewes in such doctrinal country. We have on record an extraordinarily interesting set of Notes by George Cranmer and Edwin Sandys upon Hooker's draft of Book VI of the *Polity*; they were originally intended for Hooker's consideration. And they represent admirably the general nature of the collaboration between Hooker and Sandys from the beginning of Hooker's task. They may well also give pause to those who may be inclined to underestimate the time necessary to Hooker for the completion of his task. One of these Notes indicates how sharp the line of cleavage could be between Hooker and his consultants:

> that which followeth, because it is one of the most absurd disputes that ever I read, and because it favoureth the papists in some points, if it were clean left out I should never miss it.

Elsewhere we find Cranmer desirous of inserting additional anti-Roman points of argument, and on the other hand suggesting compromise with Geneva and 'entering into a politic conference with them', a note which Sandys has marked with his cross in sign of his approval of the suggestion. Cranmer and Sandys, after all, were the children, in religious thought, of an earlier generation than was Hooker, whose thought had risen above the limited issues that in the common and narrower view separated Rome from Canterbury. Sandys was far more of a politician and a legalist than Hooker. Like Cranmer, Sandys too could not attune himself to that development of the Reformation in England which in some ways became a counter-Reformation and found its logical outcome in the High Church of Laud. Sandys was by constitution inclined to the Opposition, of which he became a pillar in James' Parliaments. But Andrewes was a forerunner of Laud. Not for him was the facile crusade against Rome, or the exposition of Puritan doctrine. The Fathers were his reading, as of Donne, and the great traditions and ceremonies of the Church Universal were his delight. Famous preacher as he was, he thought other matters of greater importance than sermons. The pomp and authority of the Bishop were one with the piety and deep devotion of the Christian man in Lancelot Andrewes.

What we have in print of Hooker's Book VI, in fact, as it ultimately came to light, consists almost entirely of what was spoken of in Chancery as a 'tract of confession'. This was almost inevitable, for it is the central point of the more general questions of penitence, confession and absolution which is the subject-matter of the book as printed. It can hardly be argued, though Keble does so argue, that this is not an integral and necessary part of the wide field proposed for Book VI in Hooker's original survey of the whole work, namely the exercise of ecclesiastical jurisdiction by lay-elders. Such a plan demanded full discussion of this special problem, in relation to the status of the consecrated priesthood. But it dealt with matters which lent themselves to very diverse shades of exegesis as between a Hooker and a Sandys, or a Sandys and an Andrewes, not only as between a Hooker and a Travers.

There can be no reasonable doubt that the Notes of Cranmer and of Sandys refer to the missing first part of Book VI, which dealt with lay-elders in a historical treatment of the priesthood, as we can readily gather from their Notes. And that part of the Book has not come down to us either in print or in manuscript. It was not completed, for Sandys' concluding Note runs thus:

Provided that you leave not out such other points touching their new officers and consistorie as are yet unhandled.

But what Cranmer and Sandys had before them was in an advanced state of composition. Sandys' last Note is a Note upon page 85 of the manuscript in his hands, and what he had was a fair copy written out by Benjamin Pullen and ready for the press, for one of Sandys' Notes refers to an error of the transcriber in the manuscript before him. We may readily therefore calculate the extent of this missing section of Book VI by comparison with Pullen's extant manuscript copy of Book V. And, once more, we are helped to understand more fully the inadequacy of three years for the completion and preparation for the press by Hooker of the last three Books of his treatise.

By now, one unimpeachable conclusion stands out, upon one of the many matters so strongly debated concerning the last three Books. The extant Book VI is authentic Hooker, if not the complete Hooker of Book VI. It is the 'tract of confession' upon which such a conflict of opinion arose.

A second conclusion is that we have in this conflict the true reason why there was an end to proposals for further publication of the *Polity* under Sandys' auspices.

But a further problem at once arises. We have Spenser's word for it that both Book VI and Book VII came to him, and to Andrewes, whether complete or not, in such a condition at any rate that they could with ease be prepared for the press. There was little or no need for Spenser to interfere editorially with Book VI, and what we have is therefore substantially as Hooker left it. But what we have in print is only the part of the Book which followed upon the 85 pages, in Pullen's fair copy, annotated by Cranmer and Sandys. What then happened to this important section of Hooker's completed work?

To answer this question we must turn away from the history of the manuscripts of the *Polity* to the history of the miscellaneous manuscripts of Hooker's minor writings. Here important and specific facts are now available from the authoritative evidence of Nicholas Eveleigh. Round about the year 1600 there came into Eveleigh's possession the manuscripts of Hooker's sermons upon the Epistle of Jude, and he kept them in his possession until, many years later, he received a 'special entreaty' from George Sellars of Corpus Christi College and Joseph Barnes, Printer to the University of Oxford, asking him to send these manuscripts to Oxford to be printed. This he did. And the sermons were duly printed, with a dedicatory epistle by Henry Jackson dated from Corpus Christi College on 13 January 1613/14. This publication, it will be recalled, was one of a series of editions of Hooker's minor works. Jackson, for example, had overseen the publication of his *Discourse of Justification* at Oxford in July 1612.

Eveleigh could not recall in what circumstances these manuscripts came into his possession. But it is impossible to doubt that they came to his keeping by virtue of his capacity as agent and steward to Sandys, even as it fell to him to attend to the business of the publication and sale of the 1597 volume of the *Polity*. All the manuscripts from Bishopsbourne, it will be recalled, after the preliminary opening of the cloak-bag and the 'general view' taken of them, were handed over to Sandys for sorting. Later on he brought them back to Churchman's house, sorted and 'divided into several parts' for delivery to Spenser, Parry and Andrewes. The minor writings were to be divided between Parry and Andrewes, and it was Sandys' business to see to their despatch. It would seem certain that he did not in fact despatch the sermons upon Jude, at any rate, to either of the destined editors. He handed them over to his man of business, probably for the time being, with a view to later despatch. And they lay derelict with Eveleigh for some thirteen years, as Eveleigh himself records. But for the revival of interest at Oxford, and at Corpus Christi College, in Hooker's remains, these sermons would probably have disappeared completely. A few more years later, and Eveleigh might have been unable to satisfy the appeal from Oxford, or it might have been impossible to trace the manuscripts to him as memories faded, even as his own had faded.

May not a similar answer be sought to the question about the disappearance of the 85 pages of Pullen's fair copy of the first part of Book VI? We know that this manuscript had been in Cranmer's hands, and had come from him to Sandys. We do not know that it went back from Sandys to Bishopsbourne, and so in due course came to London in the cloak-bag and once more into Sandys' hands, after Hooker's death. Certainly Spenser's description of the copy for Books VI and VII as it came out of the bag is hardly consistent with the appearance of 85 pages of final fair copy for Book VI. What we do know for certain is that the later part of the Book, still in the form of a draft, bearing upon the question of 'confession', was referred to Andrewes for his consideration, and that a difference of opinion arose upon it between him and Sandys. And we observe that this part, and this part only, of the Book was preserved and ultimately found its way into print, as the extant Book VI. Who could doubt, with all these facts before him, that it is to Andrewes that we owe the preservation of what thus remains? It is with the greater satisfaction, therefore, that we may turn for the certification of this conclusion to the 1648 edition of Books VI and VIII, in which the address 'To the Reader' records the origin of the copy for these books. They were in fact preserved by Andrewes and after his death passed to Archbishop Usher and from him to the printer Richard Bishop. Coleridge's suspicion was, indeed, precisely the reverse of the truth.

If Andrewes was the preserver of this as of other manuscripts of Hooker's posthumous works, may it not appear that to Sandys we owe such losses as have been sustained by posterity? It is strange to think how the many and varied accusations levelled at Mrs Hooker or at local vandals at Canterbury thus appear to turn back upon the friend of the accusers and to find their only justification in the carelessness of Hooker's own close coadjutor in his great work. Sandys was an extremely busy man, and he left a great deal of necessity to Eveleigh during his frequent absences abroad or out of London. This of itself might satisfy us upon the disappearance of the 85 pages of Book VI, in the light of what we now know concerning the sermons upon Jude, from first-hand evidence.

But there is surely more in it. Spenser's attitude in Court, and his refusal to answer the question concerning a difference of opinion, suggests serious embarrassment. Had it been merely a question whether the 'tract of confession' properly belonged to Book VI or was a stray discourse unconnected with that Book, surely there would have been no difficulty in replying. A merely technical question of editorial duty could not have troubled the principal editor. Nor could such a question, surely, have led to such a complete deadlock upon the proposals to publish the last Books. But upon a doctrinal question such a deadlock was possible enough, and such embarrassment was natural.

Keble is unable to accept the extant fragment of Book VI as properly pertaining to the main subject of the Book. The lay mind may well hesitate to challenge the authority of a great theologian. Yet one may be forced to refuse his guidance upon this question, as has already been suggested. Hooker's long discussion of confession, public and private, in the light of its history, ends with a statement of the present position of the Church of England in the matter, and asserts the 'penitential *jurisdiction*' of its ministers, and 'our power and authority to release sin'. Confession, penitence and absolution, in his view, are the safeguards of the principal means of grace, the Eucharist, and the discipline is in the hands of the appointed ministers of the Church. Nothing could be more germane than this, and other arguments in the 'tract', to the general question of the jurisdiction of the ministry, as against that of lay-elders. It is perhaps more significant that Keble describes these pages as 'a series of dissertations on Primitive and Romish Penance, in their several parts, confession, satisfaction, absolution'.[1] Here is a criticism of another kind altogether. It seems most probable that it was a criticism which Sandys also levelled at this part of Hooker's work. It echoes criticisms passed by Cranmer and Sandys upon the missing 85 pages, in which there were passages which were too 'papistical', and which Cranmer would gladly dispense with in the printed book. But what Hooker sets out in these pages was more in tune with the thought of Lancelot Andrewes. To him as to Hooker the sacramental aspects of the Christian life and of the true Church loomed larger than in the purview of Sandys or of Cranmer. Nor was there for either of them any more to be gained from such conferences with Geneva as Cranmer could still recommend. The Church had set her course resolutely, and the mediaeval Church had more to teach her than any of the new disciplines. Hooker, in his posthumous Books, was no longer the instrument of ecclesiastical policy as Sandys conceived it, even as he had long before ceased to be the disciple of Jewel. In the last resort, the pastoral and sacramental functions of the Church were more precious in Hooker's eyes than its place in an ordered commonwealth.

As for Books VII and VIII, there is no reason for doubting their authenticity, even allowing for the chequered history of these manuscripts from 1600 onwards, and for the editorial labours of Spenser and Jackson. Bishop Gauden, who first published Book VII in 1662, states that he printed it from Hooker's autograph manuscript, which is in agreement with what we have heard in Chancery. Part of Book VI, we know, had been copied out by Pullen, as far as Hooker had gone with the final version of the finished parts, which have disappeared. What survives was in an earlier state, as were Books VII and VIII, and in Hooker's own drafts. Book VII was further advanced than Book VIII, as we should expect from this general story of the writing of the *Polity*.

[1] Hooker, *Works*, I, xxxv.

Hooker, we must conceive, worked on several Books at a time, collecting and analysing material and notes, and distributing them under their relevant sections of the three Books, according to the plan long since worked out, but with some general concentration of attention upon each Book in the order of its priority. Thus the report of Spenser and the others upon the condition of the copy for these three Books is entirely consistent with a reasonable theory of the process of writing. We can dispense with any hypothesis of the completion of the writing by 1592, or of the destruction of complete fair copies in 1600. All we can allege against our possession of the authentic and inviolate work of Hooker is the possible contamination of the manuscripts by their clerical trustees between 1600 and 1648, with respect to Books VI and VIII, and 1662 with respect to Book VII. And we have been led to conceive the probability of the loss of a considerable portion of his finished work upon Book VI by the negligence or worse fault of his lay colleague Sandys. But we may well be disinclined to attribute any wilful corruption of Hooker's work to the Church and its ministers of a later generation. If we may assert that what survives of Book VI was saved by the pious zeal of Andrewes, we may also hesitate before we doubt the piety of a Jackson or an Usher, or of any others connected with the work of transcribing and preserving copies of the surviving manuscripts.

Yet there might be some excuse for thinking that there was a temptation, on the part of the High Church, to be less zealous to preserve Books VII and VIII. If Hooker's Book VI did not satisfy Sandys and Cranmer, his last two Books might well fail to satisfy those in the extreme opposing wing. Certainly, in Book VII, his position could not fortify that of the Church of Charles the Second. There is nothing in Hooker to serve as a foundation for an episcopacy by apostolic succession and divine institution; indeed his reservations upon this matter might furnish ammunition for an opposition. Yet it was the very root of doctrine in the State of King and Bishops. The whole of Keble's comment upon this Book shows a certain discomfort. And the contents and arguments of Book VIII would have been far from contenting James the First, much less the Tory Church of 1660.

Books VI and VIII were first printed in a year when the Monarchy and Episcopacy were falling, when England was upon the threshold of a Dissenting Commonwealth. The last three Books were printed together for the first time, in the next edition of the *Polity*, in Gauden's edition of 1661–2, early in the Restoration, with an assertion of their authenticity. And it was then that steps were taken to cast the strongest discredit upon these Books, in Walton's *Life*, which he was commissioned to write by Archbishop Sheldon. This *Life*, prefacing all future editions of the *Polity*, beginning with that of 1666, prepared the reader's mind for resistance to doctrines and positions which were suspect and which might represent, not the thought of the great apologist of the Church, but the corruptions and substitutions of her enemies. Once more, therefore, the safety and reputation of Hooker's work had been imperilled by falling into 'great hands'. At the worst, surely, advantage was taken of a mass of floating tradition and evidence, most cherished and best recalled by Cranmer's family, to serve the aims of high policy and, it may well be, in all sincerity. But it is no easy task to rehabilitate Hooker's work, after an attack from so friendly and authoritative a source, so long received as founded upon authentic history.

§ iv. THE AUTHENTICITY OF HOOKER'S *MISCELLANEA*

Much has been written, especially by Keble, that loving and acute student of Hooker, upon the criterion of style as a clue to the vexed question of authenticity in Hooker's posthumous writings. He comes to his own conclusions in several instances, upon plausible grounds. Others may be led to different conclusions by a similar process. Some may feel, for instance, that Book VII of the *Polity* reveals a mind and spirit that on occasion falls below the high and level flight even of the Preface to the *Polity*, when Hooker cannot escape the dust of controversy. Here he seems to stumble at times into the rougher paths of abuse and cruel sarcasm which are so sadly familiar in the common run of controversialists of the age. It would perhaps be well to indicate that such internal evidence must now, in certain of the minor writings also, give way to the certificate of fact.

The cloak-bag from Bishopsbourne, for instance, included among its more miscellaneous contents material for Hooker's defence of his work against the *Christian Letter*, and the manuscript at Trinity College, Dublin, is authenticated as in the main at any rate a genuine relic. So also the *Letters* to Reynoldes, contained in Keble's Appendix III, are vindicated by the reference, hitherto unexplained, to 'Benjamin', in the second letter. We now know who Benjamin Pullen was, and how important was his function in the service of Hooker and his work. The *Sermons upon Jude*, finally, have also aroused Keble's grave suspicions. But they are specifically mentioned by Nicholas Eveleigh, and their history related by him in detail. They are finally vouched for.

The question of style, raised by Keble, may well be considered in relation to Hooker's letters to Reynoldes and to the last three Books of the *Polity*. The stately dignity and the elaborate measured flow of Hooker's finished writings upon his great theme, ready to be set on permanent record, were not one with the more colloquial, more natural, more personal manner of his less premeditated, less formal work. Hooker could after all write to Reynoldes thus:

a phrase than which I dare saie Heliodorus hath not a sleeker and a trickshier one. But were it not trow you a great deal better to have fewer tongues and a little more wisdome to guide them? For any thing I can discern by this small bit of write his judgment in things and wordes are much about one pitch.

And he is also the man who could say in a sermon and set it down in writing:

> How suddenly they pop down into the pit.

He could none the less in those sermons at Bishopsbourne rival the emotional eloquence of Donne, stirring the soul as potently as he could persuade the intellect:

> If I break my very heart with calling upon God, and wear out my tongue with preaching: if I sacrifice my body and soul unto Him, and have no faith, all this availeth nothing.

In the second sermon upon Jude we may see the beloved figure stooping in the pulpit to say his word to his congregation, turning from one group to another in intimate address, from the young men to the fathers, to the matrons and sisters, and to the little ones too, with great tenderness:

> Sweet Babes, I speake it even to you also.

Here is the pastoral Hooker, the shepherd of his flock, moving more easily than in his singing-robes, no longer the disembodied voice of the Church, but a warm and living man, father, husband, friend, no less than cleric and theologian. Here we may find also the authentic Elizabethan Englishman, who could declaim with passionate patriotism concerning that which

> hath caused no small number of our Brethren to forsake their Natiue Countrey, and with all disloyaltie to cast off the yoke of their Allegeance to our dread Soueraigne, whom God in mercie hath set ouer them; for whose safegard, if they carried not the hearts of Tygers in the bosomes of men, they would think the dearest bloud in their bodies well spent,

in words which recall and echo the rhetoric of the young Shakespeare in an early history play.[1]

---

[1] *3 Henry VI*, i. 4. 137–8, the butt of Greene's famous gibe at 'the only Shakescene'.

Here is, then, another Hooker, not to be bound within the limits of one mode of speech, of writing, or of being, one who is moreover not necessarily quite so humble and placid and passionless, so meekly patient as we are bidden to hold him. We may even conceive of the saintly man breaking out upon occasion into a 'Tilly vally, tilly vally, Mistress Joan', without casting a shadow upon the general contentment, peace, and good fortune of his marriage with the daughter of John Churchman.

TRANSCRIPTION OF DOCUMENTS

The transcriptions of documents have sought to reconcile fidelity to the manuscript original with typographical simplicity in a reasonable compromise. Differences of handwriting have not been represented by differences of type, except that italic type occasionally indicates the use of an Italian hand. Initial ff is printed as F, final ꝑ as s (but Rꝑ as Ris=Regis, and RRꝑ as RRis=Regno Regis), and crossed p as per, pro, etc. Deletions are indicated within the signs [ ], and interlined additions or revisions within broken brackets ⌐ ¬. Illegible passages are enclosed within the signs ⟨.....⟩. Carets have mostly been omitted. The original punctuation has been reproduced. In the *Pedigrees*, d. ⟩1593 and d. 1593⟨ signify respectively 'died before 1593' and 'died after 1593'.

Appendix A

ABSTRACTS FROM THE RECORDS OF THE COURT OF THE STATIONERS' COMPANY

The following instances from these records, mainly of printing on commission, taken from the invaluable edition by Dr Greg and Miss Boswell which covers the period 1567–1602 (London: The Bibliographical Society, 1930), furnish material for arguments contained in the text. I have added further facts, with comments.

i. 18 January 1584. Richard Day's assigns agreed to pay the printer Thomas Purfoot for printing the first sheet of the *Little Catechism* at the rate of 2*s*. 4*d*. per ream for printing only. It is stated definitely that they are to provide the paper, and this appears to be the general rule unless paper is specifically included in any price stated. The actual phrase used is 'ye first *leafe*', but you do not print a leaf: 'sheet' is surely meant. *Records*, p. 16.

ii. 15 March 1587. Ralph Newbury was authorized to reprint Bullinger's *Decades* (a collection of fifty sermons in translation). Newbury had endowed the Stationers' Company with the profits of this valuable copyright, for the benefit of the poor of the Company. He was now to print 1250 copies, which he was to sell to stationers at the price of 5*s*. a copy or 26 for the price of 25, i.e. £6. 5*s*. 0*d*. (on the principle of a double baker's dozen). At the latter price the whole edition would bring him in £300. It was laid down that Newbury should pay over to the Company £10 as profit, in the terms of his benefaction, and as much again for any subsequent edition, or in proportion for any number published above 1250.

I have collated a copy of the 1587 edition of the book thus published. It contains 155 sheets. The paper is of similar quality to that of the 1596 *Book of Martyrs* (see v. below), and may be costed at 7*s*. the ream. We may take the maximum cost of printing to be the sale price to stationers with the addition of the profit stated, a total of £310. The maximum cost of printing and working alone comes out at 22s. 6d. a sheet. This may be compared with Windet's price to Sandys, Robinson's to Harrison and Bishop for Corderius' *Dialogues*, and Short's for the *Book of Martyrs* (see iii. and v. below).

Records, p. 22.

iii. 6 July 1589. Robert Robinson contracted to print Corderius' *Dialogues* for John Harrison the elder and George Bishop, owners and publishers of the book. They were to pay him for the printing at the rate of 3s. 6d. per ream. The number of copies at each impression was to be 3000. The type was pica roman. It is clear that the cost of paper, as in i. above, was not included in the contract, which provided only for printing and workmanship. The paper was to be supplied by the publishers. In this instance, as soon as we know the number of sheets in the book, we can arrive at the cost of printing per sheet.

I have not been able to trace a copy of the 1589 edition of the *Dialogues*. But a later edition, which we may take to be unaltered in this respect and which may serve our purpose, has 31 sheets ([A] B–Z8, Aa–Hh8; octavo). Taking the ream at 480 sheets the total cost of printing 3000 copies at 3s. 6d. the ream was therefore £33. 18s. 0d., and the cost per sheet 22s. With the ream at 500 sheets the cost per sheet was exactly 21s.

The reason for estimating by the ream the charge for printing in this instance as in i. above is that these were small books printed in large numbers. The cost of the paper, it is true, did not enter into consideration. But there was a higher proportion of costs of workmanship, which was measured by the quantity of paper worked as compared with the amount of setting, than usual.

Records, p. 32.

iv. 3 May 1591. Richard Jones, having printed a new *A.B.C.* (*The Pathway to Reading or the Newest Spelling A.B.C.*), the copy being the property of Robert Dexter, in breach of Dexter's privilege, Dexter agreed to purchase 300 copies from Jones at the rate of 6s. 8d. per ream for paper and printing. The book consisted of five sheets. Dexter therefore paid Jones either £1 or £1. 0s. 10d., according as the ream was rated at 500 or 480 sheets, that is, approximately three farthings per copy.

Allowing either 2s. 4d. or 3s. 6d. for printing alone, as in i. and iii., we are left with 4s. 4d. or 3s. 2d. for paper only per ream. But this would certainly be for a very low grade of paper.

Dexter, in the circumstances, probably paid a minimum price, practically the bare cost.

Records, p. 37.

v. 7 April 1595. It was agreed that Peter Short (afterwards Printer to the University of Oxford) should complete an unfinished reprint of Fox's *Book of Martyrs*, upon which Henry Denham had been engaged. The list of subscribing partners in the publication, with the number of copies due to each as his share, gives the total number of copies in the edition as 1200. Short was to be paid, for paper, printing, working, and perfecting, at the rate of 17s. 6d. per copy. The paper, it is laid down, is to be at 7s. per ream. It is clear enough that this price of 17s. 6d. per copy was to be for a copy of the whole book, including Denham's and Short's sheets, not Short's only. The unknown factor is then the number of sheets for which the partners were giving 17s. 6d. per set, the paper being of the quality that costs 7s. a ream. Short's 1596 edition of the *Book of Martyrs* contains 552 sheets.

The cost of paper comes to £463. 15s. 0d., and the cost of printing £580. 5s. 0d., of the total of £1050 paid to Short. The cost of printing then works out at 21s. per sheet. The book, it will be noted, has many illustrations, and a good deal of printing that is complicated in lay-out, to say nothing of special founts required, e.g. an Anglo-Saxon fount.

I have examined the 1596 edition carefully with a view to finding indications of the change of printer, but without success. It seems clear that the same printing-house printed the whole work; at any rate the same founts and ornaments recur throughout. Nor can I find any other indication to give a clue.

Short was to have his profit by being allowed to print 150 additional copies at his own expense, to be sold for his benefit along with the others. He became a partner, in effect.

Records, p. 51.

vi. 19 January 1598. The Court of the Company took action 'against the excessive price of books', and fixed normal prices for the future. For books without illustrations the price was not to exceed 1*d.* for two sheets in pica, or 1*d.* for one and a half sheets in brevier and long primer.

It is evident that we are here concerned with prices to be charged by booksellers to the public. We cannot therefore use this criterion to estimate costs of printing or production without allowing for the bookseller's profit or commission. If Short, for example, sold 552 sheets of the *Book of Martyrs*, the selling price would work out at 23*s.*, leaving a margin of 5*s.* 6*d.* over the 17*s.* 6*d.* paid to him as printer. But this was, in fact, an illustrated book. The margin is 31½ per cent.

Newbury's *Decades*, again, with its 155 sheets, could be sold at 6*s.* 5½*d.* or 6*s.* 6*d.* by the stationers to whom it was distributed at 5*s.*, a margin of 30 per cent. This was not an illustrated book.

If now we apply these indications to the *Ecclesiastical Polity*, we find a selling price for 53 sheets to be 2*s.* 4½*d.* Taking away from this a margin of 30 per cent, we arrive at 1*s.* 8½*d.* as the cost price. The cost of 1200 books at 1*s.* 8½*d.* is £102. 10*s.* 0*d.* They actually cost Sandys £100. 14*s.* 0*d.*, or without his payment to Hooker for the copy £90. 14*s.* 0*d.*   *Records,* pp. 58–9.

vii. 26 March 1599. Markham's *Book of Horsemanship* was printed by James Roberts on behalf of William Wood, who was to pay Roberts for the printing at the rate of 8*s.* per ream for paper and printing, for the whole edition. We may assume here the normal edition laid down by regulation, an edition of 1250 copies. This is a close parallel to iv. above. It will be observed that most of these transactions concerned books of a popular and cheaper sort, involving neither fine or expert printing nor fine paper.

viii. 19 January 1598. I add here a transcript of the order against printing for persons who are not stationers. The Company evidently took a serious view of transactions which in effect brought outsiders into their trade to share its profits.

19 Ianuarij

Against printinge for forens to the Company   Forasmuche as divers abuses, of late tyme have ben Committed by sundry persons of this Companye in procuringe of Copies and Books to be entred and alowed unto them and then pryntinge the same for

suche persons as be not of this Companye For Remedie thereof,
Yt is ordered that if any person or persons of this Companye
shall hereafter print or cause to be printed any copie or booke
whiche shall not be proper to hym self and whereof he shall
not reape the whole Benefit to his own use. by sellinge it in
the Companye but shall suffer any other person or persons that
shall not be of this companye to have the benefit of the sale or
disposition thereof. Then in every suche case all and every suche
books and copies shall and may be disposed & printed againe
accordinge to the discretion of the master, wardens, and Assistents
of this Companye for the tyme beinge or the moore parte of
them And the party or parties offendinge herein shall ipso facto
Lose & forfait all his and their Right & interest in all & every
suche booke & books.

publique   Also yt is ordered that these ordonnances against
Reading   excessive pryces of books and against printinge for
forens to this Company shalbe wrytten in the Redd booke and
publiquely Redd to this company with thother ordonnaunces on
the usuall quarter Dayes.   *Records*, p. 59.

ix. 13 August 1599. The entry concerning Henry Smyth's
Sermons runs as follows:

13 Augusti

Mr Leeke   yt is ordered by their assent. that they may sell out
Mr Burby   this Impression w^che they haue last printed (whereof
they haue about a thousand left at this p'sent vnsold) at xx^d the
booke: And that at all Impressions thereof after this, they shall
sell [it] at ij shets a peñy & not aboue Viz̃ the booke called
m^r Smythes sermons lately printed by Robert Dexter and them.

                                                   Records, p. 73.

Appendix B

EXTRACTS AND ABSTRACTS FROM THE RECORDS OF THE COURT OF ASSISTANTS OF THE MERCHANT TAYLORS' COMPANY

A. JOHN CHURCHMAN.

i. Vol. 3, f. 65a, 10 July 1581

On Quarter Day the following were elected: Master, Richard Bourne; Wardens, Richard Offley, George Sotherton, Richard Proctor, John Churchman.

'John Churchman for the fourthe and yongeste Warden.'

The election was declared in Hall at dinner the same day, after which Proctor and Churchman took the oath of office, the rest of the new officials being away in the country.

ii. Vol. 3, f. 196b, 14 July 1589

On Quarter Day George Sotherton was elected Master, and John Churchman 'first or vpper warden'.

The election was announced at dinner, after the second service, in the presence of the Lord Mayor, Lord Strange, Lord Windsor, and other guests. All four new Wardens were absent, and more severe penalties for such absences were considered.

iii. Vol. 3, f. 271a, 8 July 1594

On Quarter Day the following were elected: 'Mr John Churchman for the Mr or governor of this corporacon'; Wardens, Robert Hampson, Thomas Alderworth, Roger Helye, Thomas Juxon.

After the secret election the Company, according to the usual custom, went to church and thereafter to dinner. After the second service, when the 'tables were vpp for waters', the election was declared to the Company and its guests, including the Lord Mayor, the Earl of Essex, the Earl of Southampton, Lord Borough (or Burgh), and others. The new Master and two of the Wardens were absent, and a committee was set up to consider such contempts of the Company.

iv. Vol. 5

John Churchman made his last appearances on Quarter Day on 16 July 1604, on Audit Day on 24 August 1604, and on the Court of Assistants on 15 December 1604.

v. Vol. 5, f. 194a, 12 October 1605

And whereas it hath pleased god somuch to honor one brother of the Company as to advaunce him to the said high place of Lord Maior[1] of this honorable Cytty of London It hath neverthelesse ben his pleasure somuch to deiect and cast downe Mr John Churchman an other brother of this society (who hath passed and supplied the chief places of office in this society, namely ye places of Warden two severall tymes, and (not many yeres past) the chiefest place of Mr or Governor of this society, that nowe he is inforced to pray ayde of this society for his relief in his old age and later daies It hath therefore pleased the Company to graunt vnto him a pencon of Twenty Marcks per annū, only during the pleasure of this howse, And that there shalbe paid vnto him in hand, Three pownds six shillings and Eight pence, for Michaelmas quarter yt is past, And ye same xxty Marks per annū to be paid and deliuered him, yt it may be ymployed for his relief and mayntenaunce, & not converted to any other vse.

Margin. A pencon of 20 Markes per annū graunted Mr John Churchman a decayed Mr of this Company.

vi. Vol. 5, p. 203, 18 December 1605

At this Court the Company being moved wth greate Comisseration of the misery fallen vpon Mr John Churchman a late Maister of this Company. It hath pleased them to increase his pention from twenty marks vnto the some of Twenty pownds per Annum, the first payment to begyn at Xrmas next, and to haue contynuance only during the pleasure of this Company.

[1] The Lord Mayor in question was Sir Leonard Halliday.

vii.   Vol. 5, p. 452, 23 May 1610

Whereas the place of one of the Companies Almesmen, is lately fallen void by the death of Garson Hills, there resorted to this courte, Mr John Churchman, an auntient brother of this Company, who aboute fyfteene yeres past did supply the place of Mr or Governor of this fraternity, and being growne into decay became an humble sutor for the said place of an Almesman And with a geñall, and free consent, the same was graunted vnto him, with all allowaunces, therevnto belonging, with this further favor, that he shall contynue[1] hold and enioy his penc̃on of Twenty poundes per anñ, which the company formly graunted and allowed him, And albeit God hath laide this afflic̃on vpon him, yet by reason he hath byn Mr of the Company, It is agreed that the Almesman gowne allowed to him, shalbe made without any Cognizaunce, And that he shall not be enioyned to come to the hall, with other penc̃oners, but at his owne pleasure, nor such services be required from him, as from the rest of the Almesmen, Only he is enioyned, to frequent the Church, and to pray for the prosperity of the company, which he hath faithfully promised to performe, And also is content, so long as shall please the Company, to permitt and suffer Roger Silverwood, Clark of the Batchelers company and his wief to Cohabite with him, in the howse allotted him, in the said Almeshowse, and where, the said Roger Silverwood, by former allowaunce, and favor of the Company, dwelled by reason that Garson Hills, the former Almesman, was decayed in his sences, and not fitt to inhabite there.

Margin. John Churchman Elected an Almesman.

(At this meeting of the Court, Andrew Osborne and Francis Evington, among others, were present.)

viii.   Vol. 7, p. 45, 17 June 1612

The Almshouses were in Threadneedle Street, adjoining the Hall of the Company. A second set of almshouses, for widows of brothers of the Company, was built on Tower Hill in 1588.

In June 1612 one of the almsmen in Threadneedle Street, possibly old John Churchman himself, made a petition to the Company, as a result of which the Company provided the almsmen with penthouses 'over their heads where they vsually sitt in the streets, neere their dore, to the end they may sitt dry and warme, in colde and foule weather'.

[1] sic.

B. ROBERT CHURCHMAN.

i. Vol. 7, p. 435, 22 November 1617

On this date Robert Churchman was elected Beadle of the Company. The vacancy arose by the death of Nicholas Hurdis, and Robert was chosen out of nine candidates, eight merchant tailors and one draper, 'all proper comely men'. Robert was admitted to the office, and was also elected to the livery, and took the oaths proper to both these functions. Widow Hurdis was permitted to stay in the Beadle's house until Christmas and, if necessary, until Shrovetide.

ii. Vol. 9, p. 195 (28 August 1619, see vii. below)

Churchman was granted an addition of £4 per annum to his salary for safeguarding securities lodged against loans made by the Company.

iii. Vol. 8, p. 40, 11 May 1621

Churchman on this date petitioned the Company, urging that his expenses as Beadle exceeded the income of his office. He therefore proposed to augment his receipts by a capitation grant of one shilling out of the noble (6s. 8d.) paid by every freeman upon his admittance, and of twopence out of the half-crown paid to the Company upon the binding of every apprentice. This typical proposal of a Jacobean official was not accepted by the Company, who 'thought it not fitt'. They ordered, however, an addition of £10 per annum to his salary for the better maintenance of Robert, his wife and family, as from Midsummer. They laid down the condition, accepted by Robert, that 'he will make no further requests to the Company'. Nor was it to be a precedent.

iv. Vol. 8, f. 257b, 20 June 1625

Churchman has recently been visited by God with a grievous and tedious sickness. The Company therefore, for his encouragement, made him a free gift of £10.

v. Vol. 8, f. 288a, 17 January 1627

Upon a petition from Churchman, the Company, to encourage him in the performance of his duties, and for the better comfort of him, his wife and children, made to him a free grant of the lease of a messuage in Cornhill, formerly granted to George Smith, and now occupied by Caleb Whitfeild, for 21 years at a rent of £10 per annum. The lease was sealed on 14 February (Vol. 8, f. 289b).

vi.   Vol. 8, f. 325a, 28 May 1628

The Company was moved on behalf of Churchman to provide him with an assistant, on account of his age and his bodily weakness, which made it difficult for him to deliver summonses. The Court made a grant of £5 per annum to provide pay for an assistant, and appointed Robert Farr to the office. (Churchman was then 59 to 60 years of age.)

vii.   Vol. 9, p. 195, 13 April 1644

On this day the Court elected a new Beadle, upon the death of Robert Churchman.

William Bayley was elected. He was allowed to keep the grant of £4 per annum granted in 1619, but not the special grant of £10 per annum granted to Robert in 1621, nor that of £5 per annum granted to provide an Assistant to the Beadle.

(It is clear that Robert Churchman was a privileged and an expensive Beadle to the Company.)

Appendix C

DOCUMENTS

I. ABSTRACTS FROM PARISH REGISTERS

(a) ST AUGUSTINE'S AT PAUL'S GATE

i. *Christenings*

1575	Katherine Churchman, daughter of John Churchman	30 July
1576	Elizabeth Churchman, daughter of John Churchman	30 November
1578	Anne Churchman, daughter of John Churchman	1 May
1579	Mary Churchman, daughter of John Churchman	30 August[1]
1580/1	Sara Churchman, daughter of John Churchman	15 January
1585	Frances Evington, daughter of Francis Evington	15 August[2]
1586	Elizabeth Evington, daughter of Francis Evington	18 December
1588/9	Richard Hooker, son of Richard Hooker	19 February
1589	Katherine Evington, daughter of Francis Evington	9 September
1590	Alice Hooker, daughter of Richard Hooker	10 May
1591	Cecily Hooker, daughter of Richard Hooker	21 April[3]
	John Evington, son of Francis Evington	12 September
1592	James Evington, son of Francis Evington	10 September
1596	John Churchman, son of John Churchman the younger	11 June
	Edwin Hooker, son of Richard Hooker	21 June
1597	Robert Churchman, son of John Churchman (the younger)	3 July
1599/1600	Robert Pullen, son of Benjamin Pullen	17 February
1601/2	Benjamin Pullen, son of Benjamin Pullen	7 March
1603	Mary Pullen, daughter of Benjamin Pullen	5 June

ii. *Marriages*

1575	Francis Evington and Margaret Sandys	19 May[4]
1581	William Newcombe and Agnes Sandys	23 October
1582	John Baker and Joan Churchman	27 May
1587/8	Richard Hooker and Joan Churchman	13 February[5]
1589/90	Robert Smyth and Alice Churchman	30 March
1604	Thomas Harrison and Frances Evington	28 October

[1] Mary Churchman married Robert Cutt or Cutts.

[2] Francis Evington was born in 1549–50, being sixty-two years of age on 16 April 1611 (c. 24/366/List *v*. Osborne).

[3] Cecily Hookar   Cecily Hookar daughter of Richard Hookar was baptized the xxj daie of Aprill.

The exceptional marginal reference occurs several times in relation to entries concerning the Churchmans and Hookers.

[4] The name in both entries is spelled 'Sandy'.

[5] Hookar and   Richard Hookar and Johan Churchman were married the Churchman   xiij[th] daie of ffebruary.

The marginal entry indicates the importance attached to the event.

iii. *Burials*

1582	Alexander Sandys	25 August
1583	William Churchman, son of John Churchman	23 August
1583/4	Sara Churchman, daughter of John Churchman	19 February
	Katherine Churchman, daughter of John Churchman	22 March
1590	Margaret Churchman, daughter of John Churchman	20 November
1594/5	Katherine Evington, daughter of Francis Evington	16 January
1601	Alice Churchman, wife of John Churchman the elder	8 September[1]

NOTE. The above Abstract deals only with entries concerning Hooker's family and connections. Among other entries of interest, we find several concerning the family of William Byrd the musician, from 1559 onwards. John and Richard Langley, Thomas Butter, John Harrison, and several Aldridges, are of interest. Michael Bryskett figures in the list of burials on 23 December 1612:

Michaell Bryskett, sojourning in the house of Mary Hawley widow.

In 1566 the burial is recorded of Arthur Wyatt, son of Sir Thomas Wyatt, Knight, on 7 December, and that of Edward Wyatt, Esquire, on 25 August 1571.

In 1603 the register makes the grim observation opposite a form of cross 'Initium pestis in hac parochia', and the list of burials swells fearfully. Some measure of its severity may be found in the comparison of a list of burials for that one year, covering 5¼ pages, with previous lists covering about ¾ of a page to a year.

(b) ST ANDREW'S, ENFIELD

i. *Baptisms*

October 1592

1592, 1 October	1. Jane Huker filia Richard bapt.

Maye 1602

1602, 12 May	Marie kutts the daught of Robert gent of London baptizatus erat	12 daye

March 1602

1603, 6 March	margret churchman filia Robart baptizatus	vj daye

ii. *Marriages*

August 1561

1561, 31 August	willms stratforth et Jonā Carter nupti erāt	31 die Augusti

October 1589

1589, 5 October	Robt Smyth et Jane Stratforth

[1] Allice Churchman, the wife of John Churchman the elder was buryed the viijth day of September.

August 1597

1597, 1 August   Anthonie Stratford et Eliz churchman   1

November 1597

1597, 24 November Robert Carter et Annis Stratforde   24

December 1601

1601, 1 December Robart Cutts & Marie Churchman nupti fyrst daye

October 1616

1616, 17 October   Edward Baker of London et Frauncis Harrison widdow daughter to M^{ris} Evington   17

1629, 4 October   Rich. Cuts & Eliz. Fisher

iii. *Burials*

Feabruary 1588

1589, 2 February[1]   Richard Hoocker filius H. Se.   2

October 1594

1594, 25 October   A child of Richard Kempton dwelling within Mr Churchmans house unbapt.   25

July 1597

1597, 22 July   Edwine Hooker filius Richard sep.   22

(*c*) INSCRIPTION ON A TOMB-STONE IN THE PARISH CHURCH, CHIPSTEAD, SURREY

Here Lyeth in terred the
body of Alce Hooker eldest
daughter to the Reverend father
in God Richard Hooker Doctor
in Divinity and Dean of Sarum[2]
who departed this life the...[3]
of December Anno Domini

1649

[1] This entry probably lacks the second digit of the date. Richard was baptised at St Augustine's on 19 February in the same year.

[2] I know no authority for this statement.

[3] W. Bruce Banner, in his *Parish Register of Chipstead*, 1909, was then able to read '20' December.

II. *TRANSCRIPTS AND ABSTRACTS OF LEGAL PROCEEDINGS*

i. The History of *The Laws of Ecclesiastical Polity*

Transcript of Proceedings in Hooker *v.* Sandys

C. 24/390/100; C. 24/394/73

Interrogatories ministred by Sr Edwin Sandys knight defendant for Examination of his witnesses in the matter depending at issue between him & Alice Hooker Cicelie Hooker & Elizabeth[1] Hooker Complainants

Johēs Churchman iur 7º Julij 1613 *Mat. Carew*
Johēs Bill iur: 26 Januarij 1613 *Mat Carew*
Johes Spencer iur 26 Januarij 1613 *Mat Carew*
Robtūs Churchman iur 29º Januarij 1613 *Mat Carew*
Will̄ms Stainsby iur 7º Februarij 1613 *Mat Carew*
Nichas Eveleigh iur 6º Junij 1614 *Mat Carew*
Edmundus Parbo iur 3º Junij 1614 *Mat Carew*

1 Imprimis doo y^u Knowe the Plaintifes & defendant: & did y^u knowe one Mr Richard Hooker the Complainants father, beeing the author of the printed woork intituled Of the Laws of Ecclesiasticall Politie Eight books. And doo y^u knowe one Mr John Churchman of London Grandfather to the Plaintifes.

2 Item doo y^u knowe or haue y^u credibly heard at whose charges the first Fiue books of the said Eight books were printed, and what agreement was between the said Mr Hooker & this defendant concerning the printing of the said woork or anie part thereof. And vpon what occasion this defendant vndertooke to be at the charges of printing the said woork.

3 Item doo y^u knowe or haue y^u credibly heard who was the Printer of the said first fiue books of the woork aforesaid, & whether or no he was of kinne to the said Mr Hooker, & for

---

[1] = Margaret. See Pedigree, p. 188.

whose vse he so printed the foresaid books. And whether doo y^u knowe or beleeue that the Indenture in paper now shewed y^u intituled Articles indented agreed vpon between John Windet Citizen & Stationer of London on the one partie, & Edwin Sandys of the Middle Temple London Esquire on the other partie, bearing date xxvj^t of Januarie xxxv^th of Elizabeth, were made between the said Printer & this defendant.

4   Item doo y^u knowe of whose handwriting the said Indenture was, & whether that he wch wrate the said Indenture were the same partie wch the said Mr Hooker did vse in writing out of the said books, & what was the name of the said partie: And whether doo y^u knowe the parties whose names are subscribed to the sealing & deliuerie of the said Indenture. Or wch of them doo y^u knowe, & whether are those names of the true hand-writing of the same parties as y^u knowe or beleeue. And whether doo y^u knowe or beleeue that the part of the Indenture now shewed y^u was sealed & deliuered by the said John Windet yea or no.

5   Item doo y^u knowe or haue y^u credibly heard, that this defendant gaue anie monie to the said Richard Hooker for the grant of the Copie of the said woork to be printed as aforesaid. And how much was the said monie, & who paid the same, declare y^or whole knoweledge therein. And likewise how manie printed copies of the said first fiue books were giuen by this defendant to the said Mr Hooker in recompense of the woork & grant aforesaid.

6   Item doo y^u knowe or haue y^u credibly heard what price was set vpon the said printed fiue bookes by the defendant. And whether anie more were ever answered to the said defendant then Two shillings six pence a peece for the first fowre books, & Three shillings for the fift booke. And how long were the printed copies of the said books in selling as y^u knowe or haue heard.

7   Item doo y^u knowe or haue y^u credibly heard by what means or by whose falt anie of the written woorks of the said Mr Hooker were lost or perished after his death. Declare y^or whole knoweledge therein at large.

8   Item doo y^u knowe or haue y^u credibly heard that the writings of the said Mr Hooker after his decease were committed by his Executrix into the hands of the now L. Bishop of Elie, the now L. Bishop of Worceter, Dr Spensar, & this defendant, to be dis-

posed by their common consent as they should think fittest. Or what else doo y^u knowe or haue y^u credibly heard concerning the same.

9   Item doo y^u knowe or haue y^u credibly heard that this defendant did soiourn at the house of the foresaid John Churchman. And for how long tyme & how long since was the same. And whether this defendant departed from thence not paying anie thing for his boord. And whether did or dooth the said John Churchman account this defendant to be oweing to him for the said boord, or hath he ever demanded paiment of this defendant for his said boording, declare the trueth of y^{or} knoweledge therein.

10   Item doo y^u knowe or haue y^u credibly heard of the decay in state of the said John Churchman, & of the cause thereof, & how long since the same hath happened. And whether that this defendant or his frends were anie cause or meanes of the said decay.

11   Item doo y^u knowe or haue y^u credibly heard what wealth or substance the said Mr Hooker at his death left to his wife & children. To what value did the same amount. And whether was the decay of the said John Churchman anie cause of losse to the said Complainants in their portions left wth him or wth his son Robert Churchman.

12   Item whether doo y^u knowe that the said John Churchman at anie tyme requested this defendant to entertain one of the said Complainants into his house, & what answer had the said John Churchman from this defendant, & what performance thereof ensued.

13   Item doo y^u knowe or haue y^u credibly heard who prosecuteth this present suite against the defendant in the Complainants names. And what cause hath moooued him so to doo. And from whom he hath receiued encouragement or otherwise to prosecute the same.

14   Item doo y^u knowe or haue credibly heard vpon what occasion this defendant first vndertooke the printing of the said woork of Mr Hooker at his charges And whether the said Mr Hooker were not refused before by diuers of the Stationers in Poules Churchyeard to print the said woork at their charges for feare of losse by the same.

7 Julij 1613. A° RRis Ja: 11°/   Ex parte Edwini Sands Militis
def. versus Aliciã Hooker et
al quer Testes exam per Othon
Nicholson in Canc Exaiator/

JOHN CHURCHMAN Cittizen and Merchantailo^r of London of
the age of 90. yeres or therabts sworne &c. 1 Inter That he
knoweth Sr Edwyn Sands kn^t the def^t and allso knoweth Alice
Hooker Cecily Hooker and Elizabeth Hooker the Complts and
dyd allso knowe Mr Richard Hooker decessed late Author of
the booke of the Lawes of Ecclesiasticall Politye and saith that the
sd Mr Richard Hooker dyd mary wth this depts daughter who
was the mother of the sd Alice Cecely and Elizabeth the now
Complts and further saith that he this dept ys the same John
Churchmã of whome mencon ys made in the Inter.

3   That he hath herd that the sd booke of the Lawes of Eclesiasticall
Politye Conteyned eight severall bookes and hath allso herd that
the same was printed by one John Wyndett whoe (as he hath
likwise herd was of kyn to the said Mr Richard Hooker. And
he further saith that his name John Churchman wch ys subscribed
as a wytness to the sealing and delyvery of the writing of articles
Indented nowe shewed to this dept bering date the .26. day of
January in the 35 yere of the reigne of the late Queene Elizabeth
of happy memory ys of the proper hand wryting of this dept
And saith that he doth verely beleiue that the sd Indented Articles
were sealed & delyvred by the partyes to the same for he saith
that ells he would not haue subscribed his name thervnto as a
wytnes.

4   That Beniamen Pullen whose name ys subscribed as a wytnes
to the sd Articles indented now shewed to this dept was abowte
the tyme that the sd Articles bere date servant to this dept And
allso saith that as he verely beleveth the sd Beniamen Pullen was
the man that wrote owte the sd Mr Hokers Bookes faire. But
whether the sd Articles indented were of the sd Pullens hand
writing or not this dept saith he Cannot now depose having
Clene forgotten the sd Pullens manner of writing. and further to
this Inter he Cannot depose more then he hath deposed alredy
to the next p^rcedent Inter

7   That the writings of the said Mʳ Hooker were (as this dept rembreth) lefte at the tyme of the sd Mʳ Hokers death wᵗʰ his Executrix the daughter of this dept But how any of the sd writings were loste or w⟨......⟩ this dept saith he Cannot Certenly depose of his now rembrance

9   That the now deft Sʳ Edwyne Sandys dyd longe sithence soiourne wᵗʰ this dept, ⟨......⟩ how manye yeres this dept hath forgotten and saith that he dyd never accounte the deft to owe this dept anye thing in respect of the sd defts so souiorning¹ wᵗʰ this dept neither hath he this dept ever demanded anye thing for yt of the sd deft at anye tyme synce the defts departing from this depts howse but what the deft payd or to whose hands he payd yt this dept sayth yt ys now quite owte of his remembrance.

10   That neither the sd deft nor anye of his frends were anye Cause of this depts decaye for he saith that the same grewe Chefely by the greate losses wᶜʰ befell this dept during the late troubles in the Relme of Ireland, and partely allso by the losses wᶜʰ he had in other places where he traded.

11   That he thinketh the now Complts had no losse by this dept but that notwᵗʰstanding his decay they had all theiʳ due truly paid them by this depts sonne Robert Churchman. and further to this Inter this dept saith he Cannot depose.

12   That the deft Sʳ Edwyne Sandys at this depts request dyd place Cecely Hooker one of the Complts wᵗʰ owld Mʳⁱˢ Sandys the defts mother wᶜʰ this dept toke for a greate kyndnes and more to this Inter he Cannot depose.

13   That he verely thinketh that this sute ys followed by John Huntly a kynsman of the Complts in theiʳ behalf. And saith that he this dept hath told the sd John Huntly that if he would be advised by this dept he should geue over the sute for this dept thought he would doe [not] noe good in yt or words to the like effect And more &c/

                                        John Churchman

Capt coram Nichõ Roberts
in absenc Mⁿ̃ Nicholson/

26 Januarij 1613. Aº RRis Ja: 11º/   pro Sands Milite

JOHN BILL of London Stationer dwelling in Paules Church yarde of the age of 37. yeres or therabts sworne &c vppon the 1. 6. and 14 Inters

                              ¹ sic.

1   That he knoweth S^ir Edwyn Sands kn^t the deft But doth not
well knowe any the Complts in this sute. And saith that he dyd
well knowe Rychard Hooker in the Inter named. and well
knoweth John Churchmã of whome mencon ys made in the
Inter

6   That the price wch was sett ⌐by the deft⌐ vppon the fyve
printed bookes of the Ecclesiasticall ⌐politye⌐ (the author wherof
was the sd Rychard Hooker) was fyve shillings sixe pence only. viz.
two shillings and sixe pence for the fyrst fower bookes of the
sd fyve bookes and three shillings for the fyfte booke and more
then that was not aunswered to the deft to this depts knowledg
And saith that the printed Copyes of the sd Bookes were in
selling abowte thirtene yeres as nere as this dept now rem̃breth.

14   That he [knoweth that] hath Credibly herd that dyvers
Stationers dyd refuze to printe the sd bookes at their Charges [yt]
⌐they⌐ being offred to them by the sd Rycharde Hooker and this
dept well knoweth that Willm̃ Norton who at that tyme was
[the] a principall Stationer in Paules Church yarde was one of
them that refused to print the sd bookes at his Charge for feare
of losse by the same. And more &c

John Bill

27 Januarij 1613. A° RRis Ja: 11°   pro Sandys Milite

JOHN SPENSER docto^r in divinity President of Corpus Christi
Colledg in Oxford aged 54 yeres or therabts sworne &c ⌐vppon
the .1. 3 4 5. 8. 11. 13. & 14 Inter⌐ 1 Inter. That he knoweth the
1 deft Sir Edwyn Sandys kn^t and some of the Complts but not
all And saith that he was familiarly acquainted wth Mr Richard
Hooker the Author of the printed worke intitled Of the Lawes
of Ecclesiasticall politye. And that he allso knoweth Mr John
Churchman Father in lawe of the sd Richard Hooker.

3   That he hath Credibly herd and verely thinketh that John
Wyndet in the Inter named was the printer of the fyrst fyve
bookes of the worke aforesayd and that he was of kyn to the sd
Hooker and that the sd fyve bookes were printed at the Charges
of the sd Sir Edwyn Sandys And further saith that the writing
indented purporting certen Articles agreed vppon betwene the
sd John Wyndett of the one parte and Edwyn Sandys of the other
parte and now shewed to this dept was truly made betwene the
sayd partyes to the same as this dept verelye beleveth.

4   That vppon sight of the sd Indenture and by Conferring the same wth the hand writing wth w^ch ⌐a great parte of⌐ the [originall] Copy of the sd Mr Hooke^rs bookes are written this dept ys induced to beleue that they were both written by one man whose name as this dept hath Credibly herd was Beniamen Pullen then servant to the sd Mr John Churchmã whome this dept dyd well knowe and whose name dothe appere subscribed as a wytnes to the sd Articles. But to the rest of the Inter he saith he Cannot more depose then as to the next p^recedent Inter he hath deposed

5   That he hath Credibly herd and beleveth yt to be true vppon sight of the Accompts of one Mr Nicholas Euelighe (who was sometymes this depts [Sholar] Scholar and ys brotherinlawe to the deft) wch accompt partely vppon remẽbrance and partely vppon Comparing the hand writing of yt wth other letters of his this dept verely beleveth to be written wth his owne hand) That there was twenty pounds payd in the defts behalf to the sd Mr Hooker in Consideracon of the graunte of printing the Fyfte booke of Ecclesiasticall polity And saith that he knoweth that the sd Mr Evelighe in the absence of the deft beyond the seas was the principall mannager of the defts busynesses And this dept hath herd and verely beleveth that the sayd Rychard Hooker had dyvers Copyes allowed to him in Consideracon of the sd booke but the number of the sd Copies this dept knoweth not

8   That he well rembreth that Mr Hookers papers and writings being sent vpp to London by his Executrix they were opened in the presence of his Fatherinlawe Mr John Churchmã the now Lord Bishop of Worcester, the now deft, S^ir Edwyn Sandys, and this dept, and that after a particular vew taken of them, by generall Agremẽt they were all lefte wth the deft for the better sorting of them. who afterwards vppon desyre to fytt to the print such writings as might be thought worthy to to^1 come abrode (the Choyce writings of the sd Mr Hooker wch were most desyred being kept away from ⌐this dept and the rest⌐ [vs] or vtterly perished) dyvided them betwene the nowe Lord Bishop of Elye, the Lord Byshop of Worcester and ⌐this dept⌐ [my self] who were all of inward acquaintance wth the sd Hooker.

11   That he hath Credibly herd and doth beleue that the whole substance of the sayd Mr Hooker lefte at his death to his wief and Children amounted to the sumẽ of eleven hundred pounds

¹ sic.

or therabts and that notw^thstanding the decay of the sayde
Mr Churchmã, there was Course taken that the Childrens
porcons were payd by   *By me John Spenser.*

Robert Churchmã sonne of the sd John Churchman and one
Mr Stratford his sonne in lawe.

13   That he this dept hath gathered by often talkeing wth one
Mr John Huntlye that he the sd Huntly dyd prosecute [sute] this
sute againste the deft in the behalf of the Complts.

14   That he hath long synce Credibly herd and doth beleue that
the sd Mr Richard Hooker having dealt wth dyvers Printers for
the printing of the sd Bookes & fynding none that would bere
the Charge of printing them vnles him self would geue somwhat
towards the Charge therof, because bookes of that Argumẽt
and on that parte were not saleable as they alledged, was very
much dismayed And [this dept] that the deft who was then
daily Conversant wth him having at length fyshed owte the
Cause of his malencholy dyd make him an offer to print them
at his owne Charges and to geue him a certen number of Coppies
wch the deft (as this dept hath Credibly herd) performed, with
adding of Certen moneys. wch offer the sd Mr Hooker as this
dept hath Credibly herd dyd accepte very kyndly And thus
muche this dept saith he tould to the sd Mr Huntly abowte the
begyning of this sute as he nowe rem̃breth. And more &c

                                        By me John Spenser

29º Januarij 1613. Aº RRis Ja: 11º   pro Sandys Milite

ROBERT CHURCHMAN of Fering in the County of Essex gent
of the age of .44. yeres or therabts sworne &c vppon the .1. 3. 4.

1   8. 9. 10. 11. 12. 13. Interrs. 1 Inter That he knoweth the partys
to this sute both plts and deft and dyd knowe Rychard Hooker
late Father of the Complts being the Author of the printed worke
intitled. Of the Lawes of [the] Ecclesiasticall politie [being] ⌈in⌉
fyve bookes printed And saith that Mr John Churchmã in the
Inter named ys this depts Father.

3   That one Mr Wyndítt was the Prynter of the sd worke being
the fyrst fyve bookes of Ecclesiasticall polítye and dyd somtymes
Call the sd Mr Rychard Hooker his Cousen Hooker And saith that
he dyd here that the sd worke was printed at the Cost and Charge

of the now deft but to whose vse this dept nether knoweth nor
hath herd and further saith that he dothe thinke that the wryting
indented purporting Articles of Agremẽt made betwene John
Wyndit Citizen and Stationer of London of the óne parte and
Edwyne Sands of the Myddle Temple London Esqr of the other
parte and now shewed to this dept [are] were truly made betwene
the sayde partyes to the same for that he seeth the name of one
Beniamen Pullen sett as a wytnes to the same wch name as allso
the whole wryting indented this dept verely beleveth was [in]
the proper hand wryting of the sd Pullen for that the same ys
very like his mann^r of wryting wherwth this dept was well
acquainted

4   That tuching the sd wryting indented and subscriptions therto
he sayth he Cannot more depose then as before to the next
p^rcedent Inter for he was not p^rsent at the sealing and delyvery
therof But sayth that he hath herd and doth beleue that the sd
Beniamen Pullen dyd wryte all or some parte of the sd worke
before the same was printed

8   That after the death of the sd Rychard Hoker there were
Certen wrytings brought to this depts sd Fathers then howse in
watling strete by one Philip Cullam this depts fathers servant
wch were had forth of the Countery from the Executrix of the
sd Rychard Hoker and were delyvred to the hands of M^r do^r
Pary M^r do^r Spencer and the now deft who after they had
perused the sayde wrytings dyd say that they were the vnperfect
Copyes of the other three bookes of Ecclesiasticall politye ⌈then
&⌉ yet vnprinted and [they] being then as yt semed willing to
reduce them into forme fyt for the presse they dyvyded the sd
wrytings or Copyes betwene them saying that they would
delyver some parte of them to docto^r Androwes now ⌈lo:⌉ Bishop
of Ely for him to peruse and sett in order.

9   That the sd deft dyd souiourne at the howse of this depts sd
Father John Churchmã and as this dept thinketh he was there
abowte a yere or twoe abou[e]t a dowson yeres now past in all
wch tyme this dept never knew [the] nor herd of anye thing payd
by the deft for his borde neither dyd hee this dept ever here his
sd Father accounte of anye thing to be owing to him by the
deft for his sd borde or to demand of the deft anye paymẽt for
his bording.

10   That he to well knoweth of the decay of the sd Mr John
Churchman ⌈in his estate⌉ and of the Cause therof wch hapned

abowte nyne or ten yeres past But this dept cannot saye that the deft or anye his frends were anye Cause therof

Robert Churchman

11   That he hath herd that the sd Mr Rychard Hooker at the tyme of his deathe lefte vnto his wief and Children abowte ten or eleven hundred pounds in estate and substance wherof his wief had six or seven hundred pounds and his fower Children a hundred pounds a pece or therabts. And further sayth that yt was some losse to the sd Rychard Hokers Children in their porcons that the sd Mr John Churchmã fell into decay for that yf his estate had Contynewd good he should haue geven the Children breding vpp or Consideracon for the same in regard of their porcons that were in his hands but by reson of his decay [and estate] in his estate the sd Children had only their principall money wch was payd by this dept

12   That he hath herd that the sd Mr John Churchmã dyd entrete the now deft to geue interteynemẽt [to] as a servant or otherwise to one of the now Complts and that the deft denied so to doe but yet placed her wth his mother.

13   That he knoweth that this sute for the plts ys prosecuted by one John Huntly a master of arts of Oxford against the now deft and this dept verely thinketh that the sd Huntly dothe yt for no other Cawse then only owte of the mere love that he bore to the sd Rychard Hoker and the love he now bereth to his Children the now Complts And the reson induceing this dept so to beleue ys for that in their behalf he dyd prosecute the like sute against this dept [in l] and this dept could yet never lerne that he dyd yt owte of anye malyce or for anye gayne to him self. And more &c

Robert Churchmã

7º Februarij 1613 Aº RRis Ja: 11º   pro Sandys Milite

Willm Stansby. of London Staconer dwelling at Paules Wharff of the age of 42. yeres or therabts sworne &c vppon
1   the .1. 3. 4. 6. & 14. Interrs   1 Inter. That he knoweth Sr Edwyn Sands kn^t the deft and knoweth one of the Complts And dyd knowe Rychard Hooker the author of the Printed worke intitled. Of the lawes of Ecclesiasticall Polity But doth not knowe John Churchmã in the Inter named.

3   That one M^r wynditt late of London Staconer decessed was
the Printer of the Fyve bookes of Ecclesiasticall Polity and [dyd]
the sd M^r wyndett & the sd Rychard Hooker dyd Call eche other
Cowsens and this dept thinketh that the sd M^r wynditt dyd printe
the sd .5. bokes to his owne vse for this dept knoweth not for
whose vse ells yt should be. And he further saith that he thinketh
the Indenture in paper bering date the the[1] xxvj^th daye of January
in the 35. yere of the reigne of the late Queene Elizabeth of happye
memory was made betwene the sd M^r wyndet & the now deft
Sr Edwyn Sands for that he seeth the name of the sd Mr Wyndett
subscribed to the sd Indenture w^ch ⌈name⌉ this dept doth beleue
and partely knowe to be the sd M^r wyndets hand wryting.

4   That he doth not knowe who yt was that wryt the sd Indenture
nether doth he knowe whoe yt was that wrytt the aforesd bookes
wherof Mr Hoker had the name to be the Author before they
were printed neither dothe he knowe the hand wryting of the
partyes whose names are set as wytnesses to the sd Indenture nor
Can depose anye thing of the sealing & delyvery therof.

6   That he knoweth not whoe dyd sett the price vppon the sd
bookes but knoweth that the sd M^r wyndet sold the fyrst fower
bookes for ij^s vj^d and the vth booke for iij^s wch pryce whether
yt were aunswered to the deft or not this dept knoweth not
nether doth hee now reɱber how long the printed Copyes were
in selling nor hath herd to his now reɱbrance.

14   That he knoweth not nor hath herd vppon what occasion the
deft Dyd vndertake the Charge of printing the sd bookes yf he
dyd so doe But dyd here that in those dayes some dyd denye to
deale wth printing the sd bookes because the Charge was thought
to be to greate. And more &c   *By me Willi: Stansby:/*

3° Junij 1614. A° RRis Ja: 12°   pro Sandys mil.

EDMUND PARBO of Staple Inne in the County of [kent] Midd
gent aged 43 yeares or thereabouts sworne & examined, & by
direccon vppon the 1 & 7. Inter. 1. Inter. That he knoweth
Sr Edwyn Sandys knight named in the title of the Interrs for
defendant in this suit And doth also knowe ⌈M̃⌉ John Churchman
named in the Article, And did well knowe M̃ Rychard Hooker
deceased, named in this Inter, when he was lyving, but doth not
knowe any of the partyes named for the Complts in this suit.

                          [1] *sic.*

7   That after the deceasse of M̃ Hooker named in the Article, one
Nethersole did marry wᵗʰ his wyddowe by meanes whereof
⌈dyvers of⌉ the bookes and ⌈written⌉ woorks of the said
M̃ Hooker came to the hands of him the said Nethersole And
(as this deponent hath Credibly heard [the] and verely beleeveth
it to be true) the said Nethersole one M̃ Raven the Schoole
master of Canterbury and one M̃ Aldridge Combyning themselves together did labor to subpresse the written bookes ⌈&
woorkes of the said⌉ [of] M̃ Richard Hooker, And (as this
deponent hath likewise heard) the better to effect their purpose
they the said Nethersole Raven and Aldridge did burne or cause
to be burned all or most of the written woorks of the said
M̃ Rychard Hooker wᶜʰ soe came to their hands, And this he
sayeth is as much as he can materially depose to this Inter. And
more &c.
                                                    Edm: Parbo

6 Junij 1614. Aᵒ RRis Ja: 12ᵒ   Pro Sands Milite

NICHOLAS EVELEIGH. of *Bovitracie* in the County of Devon
Esqr aged .50 yeres or therabowts sworne &c vppon the .1. 2. 3. 4.
5. 6. 7. 8. & 9 Interrs. 1 Inter That he knoweth not anye of the
1 Complts but dyd knowe Mʳ Richard Hooker named in the Inter
and knoweth the deft Sʳ Edwyne Sands and Mʳ John Churchm̃a
whose daughter the sd Mʳ Hooker married
2   That he doth knowe that the vᵗʰ booke[s] of the Lawes of
Ecclesiasticall polity written by the sd Mʳ Hooker was printed
at the Charg of the sd Sʳ Edwyne Sands ⌈then Mʳ Edwyne Sands⌉
wᶜʰ hee knoweth to be true for that duringe the tyme of the sd
Sʳ Edwyne Sands his absence beyond the Seas he this dept dyd
paye owte of the moneys of the sd Sʳ Edwyne Sandys, the money
wᶜʰ the Printer had for doing of the same. And this dept doth not
rem̃ber that ever anye man ells was nomynated at that tyme to
haue bene at the Charge of printing the sd fower former bookes
but the sd Sʳ Edwyne Sandys then Mʳ Sandys wᶜʰ he the sd
Sʳ Edwyne Sandys vndertoke (as this dept hath often heard and
doth verely beleue to be true) principally for the love and good
respect wᶜʰ the sd Sʳ Edwyne Sandys dyd then bere to the sd
Mʳ Hooker and for that the Printers at that tyme were fearfull
to adventure vppon printing bookes in that kynde for that the
bookes of a reverent man being then newly printed were badly
soulde.

3   That one Mr Wyndett was printer of the sd fyve bookes who was said to be of kyn to the sd Mr Hooker. And the sd bookes were printed to the vse of the sd Sr Edwyn Sandys wch this dept knoweth to be true, for that he payd the printer for printing of the sd fyfte booke [and receved other soȝes for ⌈from⌉ the sd printer] after the rate of xx^s for every shete therof and receved other suȝes from the sd printer both for the sayde fyfte booke and allso for some arrerages of the former fower bookes wch mony this dept receved and payd to the sd Sr Edwyne Sandys his vse and for his benefyt onlye

4   That he verely thinketh the writing indented now shewed to him to be the hande writing of Beniamen Pullen, who vsed to write dyvers writings of the sd Mr Hookers. And this dept dyd knowe the partyes whose names are subscribed to the sealing and delyvery of the sd Indenture And doth verely beleue the names subscribed thervnto to be the very hand wryting of every of the sd partyes and allso verely beleveth the sd writing to be the dede of the sd John Wyndett.

5   That he hath heard that the sd Mr Sandys gaue to Mr Hooker ten pounds for the fyrst fower bookes, but what Coppies therof the sd Mr Hooker had this dept doth not now reȝber. And he further saith that wheras the sd Sr Edwyne Sandys [had] (as yt semes by this depts letters wch he hath perused written to the sd deft abowte that matter while he was beyond the Seas) ⌈had⌉ promised Mr Hooker forty pounds for the fower later bookes he this dept (in the behalf of the sd deft dyd paye to the sd Mr Hooker xx^{li} vppon the printing of the sd fyfte booke, [refreyning] ⌈forbearing⌉ to pay the other xx^{li} till the later bookes should be published. And this dept sayth that the sd Mr Hooker had manye Copyes of the sd fyft booke ⌈to⌉ bestow[ed] vppon his frends the certen number wherof this dept doth not now reȝber being a thing done so longe synce (viz) in or abowte December .1597.

6   That he was not acquainted wth setting of the price of the sd fyrst fower bookes but (as he now reȝbreth) they were sould for ij^s vj^d a pece. And wheras this dept and the printer had purposed to sell the sd fyft booke for iij^s vj^d, Mr Hooker vppon some Complaynte made to him by ⌈some of the Company of⌉ the Stationers dyd will and order that the   *N: Euelegh*

sd vth booke should be sould for iij^s and rather then the sd booke should be sould derer, semed Contented to lose the benefyt w^{ch}

was promised to him for his paynes And more to this Inter this dept saith he Cannot certenly depose.

7   That he Cannot depose anye thing Certenly saue only that he this dept had lately in his Custody Certen written Sermons of Mr Hookers vppon Jude wch he sent to Mr George Sellar of Corpus Christi Colledg in Oxford and to Josephe Barns Printer at Oxford there to be printed at their speciall intreaty But how this dept Came by them he doth not Certenly rember the same having bene in his Custody aboue thirtene yeres [sythence]

8   He Cannot depose anye thing materiall.

9   That he knoweth that the sayd Sr Edwyne Sands after the death of his fyrst wief being this depts sister dyd souiourne at the howse of the sd Mr Churchma being (as this dept now rembreth) in the yere of o^r Lord God 1588. but how longe he contynewed there or what the sd Sr Edwyne Sandys paid for his borde there hee doth not now remeber neither that ever the sd Mr Churchma dyd Complayne that any thing was behind for his the sd Mr Sandys his dyett there wch yf yt had bene so this dept dothe verely thinke the sd Mr Churchma would at that tyme haue made ⌐it⌐ knowne to this dept and more &c

N: Euelegh

Interrogatories to be ministred to witnesses to be produced on the part & behalf of Alice, Cicilye, and Margaret Hooker Complaynants against Sr Edwin Sands knight defendant

Johes Bill   iur Octob^r 1613   *Mat: Carew*
Philipp Culme   iur 2 Novemb^r 1613   *Mat Carew*
Robtus Churchman   iur 24 Novembris 1613   *Mat Carew*
Johẽs Spencer   iur 9⁰ Feb^r 1613   *Mat Carew*

1   Imprimis whether doe you knowe the parties plts and defendant yea or noe

2   Item whether doe you knowe or haue crediblie heard that Richard Hooker late father to the Complayn^{ts} deceased did in his lief tyme absolutelye make over to the defendant Eight Bookes called Ecclesiasticall pollicye Five of the which saide bookes were set forth in the lief tyme of the Complaynants saide father, and that the saide defendant did pay to the Comp^{lts} saide father Forty poundes for the same

3   Item whether did not you having to doe with the sale of some
of the Coppies of the saide Five bookes being demanded what
shoulde bee the reason why the saide bookes did beere so highe
a price as then they did make awnsweare in theis words or to the
like effect that the proffitts of the saide bookes were for the maine-
tenance of the poore Orphans of Mr Hooker Author of the saide
bookes, and did not you ground those your wordes [vpp] vppon
some speeches formerlie deliũed vnto you or in your heeringe
by the saide defendant to the same purpose.

4   Item whether did not you about the tyme [of] Willm̃ Stansbey
the nowe printer therof had a purpose to sett forth A latter
impression of the saide Five bookes demande of the saide Stansby
in theis words or the like in effect, what reason hee had to offer
to set forth the saide impression to his owne proffitt, and did not
you withall threaten the saide Stansbye that the saide defendant
would complayne of the saide Stansby for going about to wrong
poore Orphanes in depriving of ther right and did not you ground
those your speeches vppon some words formerlie vsed to you or
in your heeringe by the saide defend^t to the same purpose or
vppon some letters sent vnto you by the saide defendant [to the
same purposẽ or vppon some letters sent vnto you by the saide
defendant] about that tyme requesting you to deliver so much
to the saide Stansbye in the name of the saide defendant

5   Item did not you report to some of your acquaintance that the
saide defendant was at the charge of maintayning all or some of
the saide Complaynants, and did not you ground that your
speech vppon some woords vsed vnto you or in your heering
by the defendant to that purpose

6   Item whether did not you knowe or haue crediblie heard howe
many impressions of the Coppyes of the saide bookes were solde
for the benefit of the saide defendant

7   Item did not you knowe or haue crediblie heard what prices
the saide defendant did set on the Coppies of the seũall impressions
sold for the vse and beholf of the saide defendant and what proffit
hath growne to the saide defend^t from the impression of the
saide [booke] Coppies so soulde for him

8   Item doe not you knowe or haue crediblie heard what number
of all or any of the Coppies of the saide impressions nowe doe
or latelie did remaine vppon the hands of the saide defend^t

9   Item whether doe not you knowe or haue credibly heard that
the vnsaleablenes of such Coppies as nowe doe or latelye did

remaine vppon the hands of the saide defendant grewe rather
from a desire of inordinate gaine by the saide Coppies in the saide
defendant, or in such who made proffit of the saide Coppies vnder
the saide defendant then out of any dislike generally taken against
the saide worke

10   Item doe you knowe or have crediblie heard what number of
written workes of the Complts fathers were imediatelie after the
death of there saide father brought vnto the house of Mr John
Churchman grandfather to the Complayn^ts and left in trust with
the saide defendant

11   Item doe you knowe or have heard what was offered for the
Compl^ts saide fathers written workes left in the Custodye of the
defendant

ROBINSON pro q
MR CLIFFE pro def

12   Item doe you knowe or have credibly heard howe long the
defendant and his familie soiorned with the Complayn^ts grandfather Mr John Churchman and what allowance he made vnto
their saide grandfather during the tyme of ther aboade there

13   Item doe you knowe or haue credibly¹ what the number of the
defend^ts family was during all or any parte of that tyme the
defendant soiorned with there saide grandfather

14   Item doe you knowe or haue credibly heard what freindes and
acquaintance of the saide defend^ts did vsuallye resorte vnto the
Complayn^ts saide grandfathers house during the tyme of the
defend^ts aboade there and were invited by there saide grandfath^r
vnto his table for the defend^ts sake

15   Item doe you knowe or have crediblie heard that the defendant
himself or his saide freindes and acquaintance did either by there
Custome they brought vnto there saide grandfather in his trade
or otherwise recompence the Complayn^ts saide grandfather for
his chargeable entertaynement of them

16   Item doe you knowe or have crediblie heard whether the
Complayn^ts saide grandfather was not much dampnified by the
great and vnnecessarie chardges he drewe vppon himself by the
entertainement of the defendant and his familie as also of the
defendants saide freindes and acquaintance during the tyme of
the defend^ts aboade there and that the Complayn^ts saide grandfather became thereby lesse able to paye them such money as was
left in trust with him for ther maintenance together with such

¹ sic.

reasonable consideracon for the same as ther saide grandfather did at the First willinglie condiscend to allowe them for the tyme hee held the saide money in his hands

17 Item doe you knowe or have credible[1] heard that the defendant did paye vnto the Complaynants grandmother M^ris Alice Churchman ten shillings by the weeke for himself and his man during the tyme of his Aboade there with there saide grandfather and that moreover hee did bestowe certeine househould stuffe of some value vppon there saide grandmother

18 Item doe you knowe or haue credible[1] heard that the imperfect draughts of the saide last three books tearmed eclesiasticall pollicye written by the Complaynants saide father and divers others his written works were deliūed to the Custodie of the saide defendant and that there was promise made by the saide defendant at the tyme of the deliūye of the saide wrytings that the proffitt that accrued out of all or anye of them should bee to the benefitt of the saide Complaynants

19 Item did not the defendant about A yeere past after some conference had betwene you and the saide defendant as touching the saide three last books assure you that the saide three last books wanted onlye but the examining that then they might bee set forth and did not as then denye the proffitt therof to belong vnto the Complaynants

20 Item doe you knowe or haue crediblie heard that the defendant was the sole or cheif meanes of the Comp^ts fathers preferment in his lief tyme and that his paines and charges in compassing the saide preferments for there saide father together with other kindnesses performed by the defendant to there saide father might well countervaile the proffit arising of the Coppyes of the saide Eight books tearmed eclesiasticall pollicye

Robert Churchman 1. 2. 9.... 10. 11. 12. 13. 14. 15. 16. 17. 18. 19, 20 & 28

Johēs Spencer 21. 22. 23. 24. 25. 26.

21 Item doe yow knowe or have you crediblie hearde howe many of the Complts saide fathers writinges or written woorkes perfecte or imperfecte were delivered to the defendt for the vse of the Complts & what they were and by whome they were deliuered to ye said defend͂

22 Item doe yow knowe or have crediblie hearde whether all or any parte of the Compl^ts fathers said ⌈writinges or⌉ written

[1] *sic.*

woorkes so delivered to the defend^t were at the tyme of the deliverie thereof fitt to be published or mighte wth some ⌐small⌐ paines from others have bene made fitt & what profitt mighte thence have bene raised to the Complts

23   Item doe yow knowe or have crediblie hearde what ⌐writinges or⌐ written woorkes perfecte or imperfecte of the Complts said fathers came vnto the hands of the defend^t or any other besides those wch were sente by the Complts said mother vnto Mr John Churchman theire grandfather & delivered to the defendt & what the said ⌐writings or written⌐ woorks were & whether all or any of the said ⌐writings or⌐ woorkes were fitt or mighte wth some small paines have bene made fitt for the presse & what profitt mighte ⌐have⌐ bene raised to the complts out of the same

24   Item did you promise about 3 or 4 yeres paste in an epistle prefixed to a latter impression of the Five First bookes called Ecclesiasticall policie, that the imperfecte copies of the Complts fathers 3 laste bookes concerninge the same subiecte showld not longe after the setting forth of the said latter impression be published to the worlde & doe yow knowe or have crediblie heard howe longe after all or any of the said coppies were fitted for the presse & doe yow knowe or have crediblie hearde the true cause why the saide coppies have bene so longe wth helde from the worlde & what perfection they have gained since there was firste promise made thereof

25   Item did you deliver vpon conference had betwene you & the Complts late governoure Mr John Huntley aboute a yere & a half paste touchinge the complts said fathers written woorkes that there was some yeres before the said conference a purpose that the said 3 latter bookes showld have bine sett forthe & that there was staie made thereof onlye by reason of a difference betwene the said defendt & the nowe lo: Bishopp of Elye about the insertinge of a tracte of confession written by theire said fathers^1 into the said bookes

26   Item did you affirme to the Complts said governo^r that the defendte was challenged ymediatlie after the deathe of the Complts said father by some of the complts Friends for carryinge awaie the profitts of theire saide fathers laboures from the complts his poore orphanns & that the saide defendt did at that tyme yeelde the benefitt wch mighte accrue out of the said books vnto the complts

27   Item doe yow knowe or have crediblie hearde that the complts

¹ *sic.*

saide fathers woorks written in maintenance of the pᵣsente governement of the Churche & hastened by such eminente persons whome the cause did moste speciallie concerne were likelie to have bredd damages to the Complts said father in the printinge thereof or must have bine suppressed had not the defendt vndertaken the printeinge of the same

28   Item did the defendt reporte vnto you since the deathe of the Complts father that theire said father sett a lower price vpon the saide Coppies of the Fyve books of ecclesiasticall pollicie then formerlie they were sold for & that after such tyme as the complts said father as is pᵣtended by the defendt had absolutelie made over the same vnto him the said defendt

3º Novembris 1613. Aº Ja: Ris. xjᵐᵒ

1   PHILLIP CULME of the parrishe of Allhallowes Breadstreet London wollen draper aged 41. yeares or thereabouts sworne & exᵈ &c. 1 That he doth know Alice, Cicylye, and Margarett Hooker named for the [defts] ⌜Complts⌝ in this suite and Sʳ Edwin Sandes knight named for the defᵗ in the title of the interr:

2   That by being servaunt vnto one Mʳ Churchman a wollen draper in London in whose house both[e] Sʳ Edwin Sandes the now deft & [the] Richard Hooker in this article named did Lye at the tyme when five bookes Called Ecclesiasticall pollicie were sett forth in the name of the sd Richard Hooker he knoweth it to be true that there was first fower of the sd Bookes sett forth & printed, & about a year after as this dept remembreth the tyme one other of the sd bookes [were] was sett forth & printed, which said five bookes were printed or Caused to be printed by Sʳ Edwin Sandes whoe had the Coppies of the sd bookes from the sd Richard Hooker, But whether the sd Richard Hooker in his life tyme did make over vnto the deft Sʳ Edwin Sandes eight Bookes Called Ecclesiasticall pollicie or whether he the sd deft did paye vnto the sd Mʳ Hooker the Complts Late father fortye poundes for the sd [Last] five bookes or noe, as in the article is supposed this dept knoweth not, nor more can materially depose to this Inter to his now present Remembraunce.

3   That he had never any thing to doe with the sale of any the Coppies of the sd bookes And is a meere straunger to any the questions in the article conteined, & therefore can depose nothing thereunto.

4   That he neyther doth or did ever knowe Willm Stansbye in the article named, neyther is he any waye acquainted with any the severall questions in this article menconed nor can depose any thing to the same.

5   That he did not at any tyme report to any of his acquaintaunce that the sd deft was at ⌈the⌉ Charge of meynteining all or some of the sd Complts neyther did he ever heare the deft vtter or vse any speeches to that purpose, nor more can depose to this Inter

6   That as he doth now remember, he hath heard that the deft
7   did sett prise of the first fower bookes being all in one volume at 3ˢ. the booke, And thinketh that the fiftth booke was likewise prised at 3ˢ. but how many impressions were made of the sd Bookes or what proffitt hath growen vnto the sd deft by reason of any the [sd] impressions of the sd Coppies, this dept saieth that he cannott declare any thing thereof eyther of his owne [knowld] knowledge or by any Credible report of others nor more saieth to these Inter or eyther of them

8   That he cannot saie eyther of his owne knowledge or by Credible report of others what nomber of all or any the Coppies of the sd impressions nowe doe or lately did remaine in ⌈or vppon⌉ the handes of the sd deft.

9   That he did never know nor heare that there was any generall dislike taken against the sd worke called ecclesiasticall pollicie whereby the same came to be vnsaleable neyther doth he knowe that the deft had any desire of inordinate gaine [by] that he would make of the sd coppies wherebye the same grew not to be so vendible as they were at the first nor further can depose to this Inter.

10   That he being servaunt to the sd Mʳ Churchman at the tyme of the death of the said Richard Hooker, was sent by the direction of the sd Mʳ Churchman whoe was father vnto the wife of the sd Mʳ Hooker, vnto Bishopsborne in the Countye of Kent at

Phillip Culme

which place the sd Mʳ Hooker was parson and dwelt there at the tyme of his death, to take a Catalogue of the Bookes whereof the sd Mʳ Hooker was possessed at the tyme of his death and Also to bring with him all such written Bookes writings & written papers as he this dept could find in the studdye & house of the sd Mʳ Hooker then deceased, which this dept did accordinglye and did putt vpp so many written Bookes, writings & written papers, as to this depts best remembraunce did fill a

Cloake bagge, [which he] ⌜And⌝ brought ⌜the same⌝ home to London to his sd Masters house, and there delivered them to the sd Mʳ Church⌜man⌝ grandfather to the sd Complts and as this dept verilye thinketh the sd deft had afterwardes the pervsing of them but whether they were left in trust with the sd deft or no this dept certeinly knoweth not neyther can he directly saye what nomber were of the sd written woorkes, neyther did he take any note of the particulars of them or any of them nor[e] more can depose to this Inter.

11   That he doth neyther knowe nor hath heard what was offred for the Complts said fathers written workes, [nether] left in the Custodye of the deft, nor further can depose ⌜to this Inter⌝. [in this behalf eyther of his owne knowledge or by Credible report of others to his now present remembraunce]

12   That of his owne knowledge the sd deft after the death of his
13   first wif did himself [and] ⌜wᵗʰ⌝ a man to waite vppon him soiourne with the sd John Churchman for the space of twoe yeares as this dept remembreth the tyme, And afterwardes the sd deft did marry with ⌜the daughter of⌝ one Mʳ Southcott, And [the] after his sd marriage, the sd deft, his wif twoe men-servaunts & one maide servaunt, did soiourne with the sd John Churchman some yeare or thereabouts as this dept taketh it. And this dept saieth that afterwardes the sd deft ⌜went to dwell in Yorkeshire where his sd wife as this dept thinketh⌝ [then wife] died, And [then the] after her death the sd deft with one man servaunt Came againe to soiourne with the sd Mʳ Churchman where they Continewed as this dept remembreth for the space of one yeare and more, but what Allowaunce was made by the sd deft vnto the sd Mʳ Churchman for any of these severall [tymes of] soiournings as aforesd this deponent knoweth not, nor more can depose to the contents of these Inter or eyther of them to his now remembraunce

14   That he doth know that many frindes and acquaintaunce did resort to the deft during his severall tymes of aboad in the sd Mʳ Churchmans house, And saieth that some tymes the sd Mʳ [Churchm] Churchman would invite them to dinner or to supper but whoe it was in particular that hath bene so invited to the sd Mʳ Churchmans table this deponent now remembreth not.

15   That he hath heard by the Credible report of others that [the sd defendt] at the decease of the defts father there was bestowed with the Complts graundfather about some twoe hundred

poundes in black Cloth for the funerall of the sd defts father but whether the sd monye was bestowed by the deft or by his procurement or no this dept certeinly knoweth not howbeit this dept saieth that if it weere so, that the sd money was bestowed with the sd Churchman by the defts meanes yett doth not this dept conceive how the bestowing of that monye or any other Custome that the sd deft brought to the sd Churchman ⌈in his trade⌉ that this dept ever heard of or sawe, could proporcionably recompence the Complts sd grandfather for his chargeable enter-teynement of the sd deft & his Companye as aforesd, if so be that the sd Churchman had no other recompence or satisfaction for the same, which if he had, it ⌈is⌉ more then this deponent did ever know or heare of:

Phillip Culme

16   As before he hath declared in the latter end of his answer to the next precedent article, That [if the] if the sd Complts grand-father was not recompenced & satisfied for the entertainment which the deft & his familie had from tyme to tyme in the sd Churchmans house, which this dept could never perceive or find in any accompt ⌈that eū he sawe⌉ that the same was dischardged by the deft for so long tyme as this dept was servaunt to the sd Mr Churchman, then this dept cannot otherwise conceive but that the sd Mr Churchman was much damnified by the great and vnnecessarye Chardges that he drewe vppon himself by the entertaynement of the deft and his familye as also of the defts frindes & acquaintaunce during the tyme of the defts aboad in the sd Churchmans house, and by that reason this deponent is induced to beleeve that the sd Churchman might become lesse able to paye the sd Complts such money as was left in trust with him for their maintenaunce, And this he saieth is asmuch as he can materially depose in this behalf eyther of his owne knowledge or by report of others vppon his now present remembraunce.

Phillip Culme.

[Respon]

24 No: Aᵒ xjᵒ Ja. Ris.   pro Hooker

ROBERT CHURCHMAN. of Feringe in the county of Essex, gent. aged 45. yeares or thereabouts sworne & exed &c

1   That he dothe very well knowe all the parties to this suyte bothe complts and the deft

2   That he can saie nothinge at all materiall to this Interr. either of his owne knowledge or vpon any report of others to his remembrance

9   That he hathe credibly hearde and dothe verely beleeve it to be true, that the vnsaleablenes of the Books of Ecclesiasticall pollicie did rather growe in respect of the greate prices & rates sett vpon them ⌐by the deft or by his meanes⌐ then out of any dislike taken or conceived against the worke it self, And this is all he saithe to this Interr. [*vide infra, Int.* 10*].

[20   That he neither knowethe nor hathe heard that the nowe deft was the sole or cheefe meanes of the compl^{ts} fathers p^rferrem^t in his life tyme. Or that any paines chardges or kindnesses done or bestowed by him the deft to or vpon the compl^{ts} sd father might or coulde Countervayle the proffitt arrisinge by the Coppies of the Eight books Called Ecclesiasticall pollicie. But Contrari-wise, this depon^t hathe very credibly heard & dothe beleeve it to be true. That he the deft was [me maner of wayes] much beholdinge vnto the compl^{ts} father for the learning and In-structions that he the deft receaved from & by him the sd Compl^{ts} father And this is all that he can saie to this Interr.

To the rest he is not exed by dyrection

Robert Churchmã]

*10   That he remembrethe that within a while after the deathe of the compl^{ts} father there weare diũse written worcks of the compl^{ts} sd fathers wch weare brought vnto this deponts fathers howse, and there ⌐weare⌐ deliũed to the now deft, but what number in certenty there weare of them, he can not sett downe onely he remembrethe that there weare as many of them as a [good] reasonable bigge Clokebagge woulde conteyne, And this is all he can say to this article

11   That he can saie nothinge.

12   That he knowethe that the nowe deft his wife childen & famely did lye and soiorne at this deponts fathers howse a good space togeither. but how longe in certenty he remembrethe not. And this depon^t neither knowethe nor hathe hearde that he the deft did paie or allowe any thinge at all vnto this depon^{ts} [for] father for the same

13   That the number of the defts famely wch did soe soiorne at this depo^{ts} fathers howse as aforesd weare some tymes 3. some-tymes 4. and sometymes more or lesse as occasion served.

14 That he knowethe it to be true that duringe the tyme that the
15 nowe deft & his famely did soe soiorne at this deponts fathers
howse, there weare diuerse of his the sd defts Frends that did
many tymes come thither vnto him ⌐the deft⌐ and weare entreated
to dyne or supp there before they went And this depont neither
knowethe nor hathe heard of any recompence, that either he the
sd deft or his sd Frends did euer give or make vnto this deponts
father for theire sd enterteynmᵗ. Nor more can saie to these
2 Interrs

                                                    Robert Churchmã

16 That he dothe verely thincke that his this deponts father was
damnefied by the charges & expences wᶜʰ he drewe vpon himself, by givinge enterteynmᵗ to the deft, his Famely, & his Frends
as aforesaide, But whither this deponts sd father did thereby
become vnable to paie and satisfie the nowe complᵗˢ such money
as was lefte in trust with him for theire mayntenance yea or noe
this depont knowethe not. Nor more can saie to this Inter

17 That he neither knowethe nor remembrethe that he hathe
heard that the nowe deft did paie vnto this deponts Mother xˢ
by the weeke for himself and his man duringe the tyme of his
the sd defts aboade at this deponts fathers howse, or that he the
deft did moreover bestowe any howshold stuffe vpon this
deponts sd Mother, But this depont hathe hearde that the deft
vpon his goinge from this deponts fathers howse, shoulde tell
this deponts mother, that he lefte her howse better then he fownde
it by a locke wᶜʰ he lefte vpon a doore wᶜʰ locke as this depont
hearde the deft shoulde saie was worthe xlˢ. And this depont
heard, that his this deponts Mother was muche discontented at
those speeches of the deftˢ, and that the same locke was not
thought to be worthe above Five shillings, And this he saithe is
all that he can saie to this Interr

18 That he knowethe it to be true, that [vpon] ⌐after⌐ the deliũie
of the written works of the complᵗˢ fathers vnto the nowe deft
as aforesd in his awnsweare to the xᵗʰ Inter ⌐and⌐ wheareof (as
this depont hathe credibly heard & beleevethe), the imperfect
draughts of the last 3 books in the Article named weare parte)
he the nowe deft did promise, that the proffitt that accrewed and
came out of all or any of the sd written workes shoulde be to the
vse & to & for the benefitt of the nowe complᵗˢ.

19 That he well remembrethe that about a Twelvemonthe nowe
last past he this depont beinge in conference withe the nowe deft

touchinge the Three last bookes in the Article named he the deft
did then affirme vnto this depon^t that the sd last three books
wanted onely but examyninge, and that then they might be sett
forthe: assuringe this depon^t then w^thall that he the sd deft neuer
meant otherwise. but that the proffitt of them shoulde come &
be to the nowe compl^ts or woords to the same purpose. And this
he saithe is all that he can saie to this Interr

20   That he neither knowethe nor hathe heard that the nowe deft
was the sole or cheefe meanes of the compl^ts fathers preferrem^t
in his life tyme, or that any paines charges or kindnesses done or
bestowed by him the deft, to or vpon the compl^ts sd father, might
or could countervayle the proffitt arisinge by the coppies of the
Eight books. called Ecclesiasticall pollycie. But contrariwise this
depon^t hathe very credibly heard & dothe beleeve it to be true,
that he the deft was much beholdinge vnto the compl^ts father
for the learninge and Instructions that he the deft receaved from
& by him the sd compl^ts father. And this he saithe is asmuch as
he can saie to this Interr

[To the rest he is not exed by dyrection]

Robert Churchman

28   That true it is that the deft did report vnto him this dept [that]
since the death of the Complts father, that their sd father had in
his life tyme sett a lower prise of the sd five bookes of ecclesiasticall
pollicie then formerly they were sould for, but whether the
Complts father did make over the sd bookes vnto the sd deft
yea or noe this dept knoweth not, nor more nor otherwise
^rsayth he^l can materially depose to this Inter.

to the rest not exd &c.   Robert Churchmã

9° Febr. A° xj° Ja: Ris

JOHN: SPENCER Doctor of Dyvinytie aged 54. yeares or thereabouts sworne and exẽd &c.

1   That he dothe very well knowe Sr Edwyn Sandes knight the
deft and Alice Hooker one of the compl^ts and he ^rthinckethe that
he^l hathe seene the other two compl^ts but he dothe not nowe
certenly knowe them.

21   That within the compasse of one yeare as he remembrethe the
22 tyme next after the deathe of the compl^ts late father, he remem-
23 brethe that the nowe Bishopp of Worcester, him self this depon^t

and the nowe deft did all meete togeither at the howse of one Mr Churcheman here in London grandfather vnto the nowe compl^ts: At wch tyme he remembrethe that there weare brought foorthe vnto them a Clokebagge with diuerse writings and written papers. wch as it seemed had beene written by the compl^ts late father and had beene sent vp out of Kent to be sorted & perused. Of wch he saithe there weare [but] two written worcks vizt the sixt and seaventhe bookes of Ecclesiasticall pollicie, though not fully perfected. And of the Eight booke of the same subiect, there weare allsoe diuerse tracts and discourses scatteredly written but noe coherent body; And witheall there weare some written coppies of some sermons that he the compl^ts father had preached as it seemed. And he saithe that [at the same tyme] there weare allsoe some other written noates of imperfect discourses, one of them beinge as he nowe remembrethe some parte of an awnsweare to a booke that was written against him the ⌜compl^ts father⌝ And at that tyme he remembrethe that they did take but a generall viewe of the particulers and fyndinge them very disordered and confused. they lefte them withe the nowe deft to sort them to theire heads, All wch writings and written papers as this depon^t thinckethe weare afterwards brought agayne by the nowe deft and devided into seuerall partes; some parte whereof vizt those ⌜as he remembrethe⌝ that did concerne the three last books of ecclesiasticall pollicye [as he] weare deliũed vnto him this depon^t, Some other partes to the nowe reverend father in god the Bishopp of Elye; and the other partes to the sd Bishopp of Worcester, and the cause whie they weare soe deliũed and lefte withe this depon^t & the other parties, was to the ende they shoulde see if they coulde reduce them to some perfection. beinge then very imperfect & ⌜a greate parte⌝ written in scattered papers. And he saithe that of all those written worcks there weare onely the Two draughts of his [Fi] sixt & seaventhe books of ecclesiasticall pollicy and some fewe sermons. that he thinckethe withe some reasonable travell & paines might have beene made fitt

John Spenser

for the presse, though nothinge awnswearable to that perfection wch the compl^ts father entended ⌜before they shoulde have come forthe⌝. And therefore what benefit might have beene raysed thereby vnto the nowe compl^ts he knowethe not because he can not tell howe saleable they woulde have proved [beinge] And this he saithe is asmuch as to his nowe p^rsent remembrance he can materially depose to all the seuerall questions of these Interrs.

24   That it is true that there was a purpose and intencion in this depon^t and some other of the sd Mr Hookers frends, that the sixt & seaventhe bookes shoulde be [aswell] perfected as ⌐well as¬ without alteracons or addicons they might be, and soe sett foorthe. And soe likewise they had such a purpose for the eight booke, if they coulde out of such scattered papers as the same was roughly [digested] drawen in. [if they coulde out of] have brought the same to any reasonable perfection. And soe muche or to that effect he thinckethe that he did promise in the Epistle menc̄oed in the Interr. And he saithe that he this depon^t himself hathe taken some paynes in the fittinge & perfectinge of those 3 last bookes and hathe brought two of them vizt the 6th & the 7th to some reasonable perfection. though[t] not yet thought fitt for the presse, for some causes wch because he thinckethe they doe not concerne the matter nowe in question [he] vnder favour of this hon court he forbearethe nowe to sett downe. And this is asmuch as to his nowe remembrance he can materally saie to this Interr

25   That because he conceivethe that the matters questioned in this Inter doe noe wayes concerne the good of the comp^{lts}, therefore vnder favor of this hon court he forbearethe to make any awnsweare thereunto.

26   That he dothe not remember that he did affirme to the nowe comp^{lts} governor any such matter or things as are menc̄oed in this Inter. But he remembrethe that the deft cominge to heare that it was supposed that the perfect coppies of those 3 latter books weare concealed in regard that he the sd def^t was to have the proffitt of the printinge [thereof] of them he the sd def^t affirmed in this depon^{ts} hearinge. That soe as hee might be a saver in regarde of the charges that he had beene formerly at about the other books, that he for his parte woulde be well contented that the nowe comp^{lts} shoulde have the benefitt of those three latter bookes. or woordes to some such effect. And soe muche it is likely that this depon^t hathe affirmed to the gouerno^r of the nowe Comp^{lts}. And this is all he saithe to this Inter

To the rest he is not exed by dyrection

John Spenser

19⁰: octobris. 1613.   Ex parte Alicie [Cicilye] ⌈Hooker⌉ et al
   A⁰ Ja: Ris xj⁰   queren versus Ed[mundũ] ⌈win⌉ Sands
                    milt deft̃e testes examinat per Nichm̃
                    Roberts in Cancellar Examinatorem.

JOHN BILL Citizen & Stacioner of London of the Age of 37.
1 yeares or thereabouts sworne & Examined &c. 1 That he doth
   know Sʳ Edwin Sands knight named for the deft in the tytle of
   the Interr But Alice Cicilye & Margaret Hooker ⌈or either of
   them⌉ named for the Complts in this suyte he knoweth nott.
2   That he cannott certeinely saie ⌈either⌉ of his owne knowledge
   or by Credible report of others that Richard Hooker ⌈deceassed⌉
   Late father to the Complts [deceased] in this article named did
   in his Life tyme absolutelye make over vnto the deft Eight Bookes
   Called Ecclesiasticall pollicie howbeit this dept saieth that he
   well remebreth that the sd· Richard Hooker in his life tyme
   [which is about] did Cause to be printed and sett forth at severall
   tymes five bookes Called Ecclesiasticall pollicye, but whether the
   deft did [by] buye the same five bookes of the Complts ⌈father⌉
   or noe this deponent knoweth not nor more can saye to the
   contents of this Interrogatorye.
3   That he must needes acknowledge that he had to doe with
   the sale of five printed bookes of Ecciesiasticall pollicie which
   this dept Receiued from the deft, And saieth that the deft as this
   dept verilie thinketh had the same bookes from one Mʳ John
   windate a printer now deceased, & not from the sd Complts
   father. And this dept saieth that after that he had Receiued the
   sd Bookes of the sd deft, there came one Mʳ Huntley [as] to this
   dept as he now remembreth his name, and tould him that [of]
   one of the sd Ecclesiasticall Bookes which this dept had formerly
   sould to an other booke seller, [would] ⌈was⌉ sold againe by the
   sd Booke seller for xˢ as the sd Mʳ Huntley then affirmed vnto
   this deponẽt whereas this dept at that tyme sould the sd bookes
   for vjˢ a peece & vjˢ viijᵈ a peece at the vttermost, And this dept
   saieth that the sd Mʳ Huntley did then saie that the ⌈now⌉ deft
   Sʳ Edwin Sands did offer iniurye vnto the sd Mʳ Hookers
   Children in taking from them the benefitt & proffitt of their sd
   fathers Bookes [which] ⌈wherein⌉ he had taken so great paynes
   in the makeing of them or wordes to that or the like effect,
   whereunto this deponent replied that he did not knowe what
   agreement was betweene the sd Sʳ Edwin Sandes and the sd

Mr Hooker, but tould the sd Mr Huntley that he ⌐this dept⌐ did heare the sd Sr Edwin Sands the now deft saie, that the sd Mr Hooker had beene very Chargeable vnto him neverthelesse (quoth he) if any proffitt or benefitt shalbe raised by the sale of the sd Bookes he would have some Consideracon of the sd Children and bestowe something of them for the Love he bare vnto the sd Mr Hooker their sd father or wordes to the verie same Effect, And this he saieth is asmuch as he can materially depose to this Interr.

4   That about the tyme that Willm Stansbye in this article named had a purpose to sett forth a Latter impression of the sd five bookes, he this dept did demand of the sd Mr Stansbye what his Reason was that he would offer to sett forth the sd Latter impression to his owne proffitt, without the privitie and Consent of the sd Sr Edwin Sands the now deft [at which] ⌐telling him that at that⌐ tyme the sd deft had many of the sd Bookes then remaining in his handes & vnsold as the sd deft [had then tell] [did] ⌐had formerly tould to⌐ this dept which would be a great hinderaunce to the benefitt of the Children of the sd Mr Hooker if so be that he the sd Stansby should likewise sett forth the same bookes or wordes to the same purpose, which sd speeches this dept ⌐saith that he⌐ did vse of his owne accord vnto the sd Mr Stansbye being grounded vppon some former conference had betweene him this dept & the sd deft concerning the ⌐good of the sd⌐ Children, and not vppon any Letter sent vnto him this dept by the sd deft to the same purpose as in the article is supposed.

John Bill

5   That he hath reported to some of his acquaintaunce that the deft [in the] was at the Chardge of keeping of one of the Complts as the deft himself hath often tould this deponent but which of the sd Complts by name was so kept by the sd deft this deponent knoweth not, nor more nor otherwise can saye for the satisfieing of this Inter.

6   That he doth neyther knowe nor hath heard how manye impressions of the Copies of the sd bookes weere sould for the benefitt of the sd deft.

7   That the sd deft did sett the price vnto this dept of so many ⌐of the sd⌐ bookes as he this dept [had he this dept] had the selling of for the deft, at the Rate of v^s vj^d a peece of thereabouts [but] howbeit he saieth that he never att any tyme had any whole

impressions of the sd Bookes, neyther doth he knowe what proffitt or benefitt the sd deft made of any of the impressions of the Coppies of the sd Bookes, sould for him the sd deft nor more [saith] can saye to this Inter.

8   That he knoweth it to be true that the deft did make a motion in the Stacioners hall vnto the [sd Companye] master[s &] wardens & Assistaunts of the Company of Stacioners at the same tyme when the sd Stansbie had the sd Bookes vppon the presse to be ⌐re¬printed, ⌐vidct¬ that the sd Stansbye might take all those Bookes called the Ecclesiasticall pollicie then being & remaining in the sd defts handes at a reasonable Rate, which the said Stansbye refused. but what nomber of all or any of the Coppies of the sd impressions did then or now doe remaine vppon the handes of the sd deft this dept cannot certeinlye declare

9   That he doth neyther know nor did ever heare that the vnsale-ablenes of such Coppies as now doe or Lately did remaine vppon the handes of the said deft grewe rather out of a desire of in-ordinate gaine by the sd Coppies in the sd deft [then] ⌐or¬ in any other whoe made proffitt of the sd Coppies vnder the sd deft then out of any dislike taken out of the sd worke, neyther did this dept ever knowe or heare that the worke ⌐it selff¬ was [disl] ⌐ever¬ disliked of any man of sound iudgement, but allwaies holden and accompted a worke very famous and praiseworthie, And this dept saieth that there is no other cause that maketh those Coppies vnsaleable that now doe or Lately did remaine in the handes of the sd deft but Onely the latter impression printed of the sd Bookes by the sd Stansbye [neyther] And this dept doth verilye thinke that the sd deft hath not sould any one Coppie of the sd booke since the tyme that the sd Stansby printed the same ⌐anewe¬. And this is all that he can materially saie in this behalf eyther of his owne knowledge or by the report of others vppon his now present remembraunce

John Bill

ii. The Legacies of Hooker's Daughters

(a) Hooker v. Churchman and Stratford. C. 2 James I. H 10/1.
(b) Hooker v. Nethersole and Dalby. C. 2 James I. H 27/33.
(c) Hooker v. Evans. C. 2 James I. H 14/19; C. 24/362/44.
                Reports and Certificates 17. (1613).
(d) Hooker v. Huntley. C. 2 James I. H 12/44.
(e) Huntley v. Huntley, Hooker et al. C. 2 James I. H 23/37.

(a)

Alice Hooker ⎫   Robert Churchman
Cecily Hooker ⎬ versus
Margaret Hooker ⎭   Richard Stratford

i. *Bill.* 25 January 1610. To Thomas, LORD ELLESMERE, Lord Chancellor of England.

1. Alice, Cecily and Margaret, daughters of Richard Hooker, late Master of the Temple and now deceased, are under age and therefore are suing through their guardian John Huntley, Master of Arts in St John's College, Oxford.

2. Richard Hooker at his death left £400 in the hands of John Churchman citizen and woollen-draper of London, bequeathed by will for marriage portions or for the maintenance of his four daughters.

3. For the security of the payment of this legacy, John Churchman and his son Robert bound themselves to John Spenser, Doctor of Divinity, and Anthony Stratford, as trustees, in a bond of £800.

4. When John Churchman's estate fell into decay, he made over to Robert certain goods with the intention that Robert should use them for the discharge of the legacy to the daughters.

5. Robert Churchman admits that he has a liability in the matter, and has been responsible for the maintenance and education of the daughters during part of the time of their minority.

6. But Robert alleges that he is liable only for £300, stating that

    (a) On 10 March 1606 he paid £100 of the legacy, by delivering to Anthony Stratford a quantity of malt worth £100 to be disposed of in part payment of the legacy.

(b) Anthony Stratford therefore became responsible for £100 of the legacy. He is now dead, but has left ample property for his executor, Richard Stratford, to discharge this debt together with interest due.

(c) Robert is ready, as always, to pay what is due from him, i.e. £300, provided that the bond of £800 is destroyed or cancelled upon this payment.

7. These matters have been referred by the Lord Chancellor to a committee of three for report, Sir Thomas Lowe, Alderman of London, Sir Henry Mountague, Recorder of London, and James Waldron Esquire. They have certified that the facts are as stated in this Bill, and so have reported to the Lord Chancellor. Robert Churchman and Richard Stratford have been duly informed that they are to pay £300 and £100 with interest respectively.

8. Richard Stratford however refuses to pay £100 or any part thereof, and Robert Churchman refuses to pay except upon order of the Court.

9. Richard Stratford, moreover, has in his possession a bond which he conceals and withholds from the plaintiffs. It is a bond by which Edward Nethersole stands bound in £800 for the payment of £400 to the plaintiffs, according to an agreement upon his marriage with their mother, the widow of Richard Hooker. The bond was left in the charge of Anthony Stratford as trustee, and from him came to his executor, Richard Stratford, who detains it from them.

The *Bill* is signed by '*Ri. Lydall*'.

ii. *Answer* of ROBERT CHURCHMAN.

The *Answer* was sworn before MATTHEW CAREW on 26 January 1610.

1. Robert Churchman agrees to the statement of facts contained in the Bill concerning the bond in question.

2. He asserts that, of the £400 due under the bond, he has already paid £100 in March 1604, being the value of malt supplied for that purpose to Anthony Stratford.

3. He admits a debt of £300, which he is ready and willing

to pay, on condition that the bond of £800 is destroyed or cancelled, so that he is discharged from it.

4. He is willing to do all this and to abide the order of the Court without further disputing the suit.

The *Answer* is signed by '*Tho: Badger*'.

iii. *Answer* of RICHARD STRATFORD.

The *Answer* was sworn before MATTHEW CAREW on 31 January 1610.

1. The facts are as stated is so far as the bond is concerned under which John and Robert Churchman became bound to Spenser and Anthony Stratford in £800 for the payment of £400, and also for the payment of interest at the rate of £8 per cent yearly to be expended upon the maintenance of the daughters of Hooker. The bond is now in the hands of Dr Spenser, and may be consulted upon the conditions.

2. It is true that a quantity of malt was handed over as stated by the Bill, but its value was not £100. In fact, when it was sold, all care being taken to sell it to the best advantage, it realized only £74. 8s. 0d., as may be seen from the account-books of Anthony Stratford.

3. Anthony Stratford, moreover, had charges to set off against even this amount. He paid for freight of the malt. Also, when Robert Churchman refused to continue hospitality to the three daughters, and to the fourth then living, Jane, and turned them away, Anthony Stratford took them into his care. For this purpose, he used the proceeds of the sale of the malt for their maintenance, for a total period of two years less ten days. His Account-books under this item show charges amounting to £44. 17s. 4d.

4. He also incurred expenditure in proceeding in bankruptcy against John Churchman on behalf of the daughters, in order to secure their legacies. Under these two heads he claims to be allowed a total of £16. 12s. 5d.

5. Richard Stratford is willing to pay to the plaintiffs everything that is due from him to them, after allowing for all these deductions from their claim.

6. He is executor to Anthony Stratford, whose brother he is. And he is bound to deal uprightly with his estate, and to do his

duty by his brother's wife and children, though not to wrong the plaintiffs.

7. Anthony Stratford certainly left enough to pay all his debts. But most of the debt here laid to his charge should be paid by Robert Churchman under his bond.

8. The Certificate of the Committee was based on information supplied only by Robert Churchman. Richard Stratford was not ready to supply evidence and proofs. They had no power to examine on oath. He is prepared to produce evidence in Chancery. The Certificate is in error. Churchman should pay more than £300, and Stratford less than £100.

9. With respect to the bond mentioned as made by Nethersole, it is true that Stratford has in his possession a bond under which Nethersole is bound in £1200 to John and Robert Churchman to perform certain covenants contained in certain indentures, to wit, to pay £100 to each of the four daughters in the event of Nethersole surviving their mother. The date of the bond is 13 March 1601, and the date of the indenture is 12 March 1601.

Stratford found these documents among the papers of his late brother, but never read them until the present suit was begun. He has not concealed or withheld any bond from the plaintiffs. And he knows nothing about any bond of Nethersole for £800 as stated.

The *Answer* is signed '*Fr. Harvey*'.

NOTE. Further information concerning the Stratford family may be found in *Star Chamber Proceedings* 8. 266/24, in which Anthony Stratford is suing John Stratford in May 1617 concerning family matters. The Stratfords were a numerous Gloucestershire clan, from Temple Guitinge and Farmecote. Anthony was a salter in London until he retired back to Temple Guitinge. His brother George, of Farmecote, was a man of means, who left £2000 at his death. His nephew Henry, though of weak intellect, was pressed for a soldier under Captain Shackerley, and was at the 'hot siege' of Ostend where, his commander subsequently said, most of his men were killed, and Henry among them.

(b)

Hooker v. Nethersole and Dalby

Bill of ALICE, CICELY and MARGARET HOOKER, dated 13 October 1610.

Richard Hooker at his death left an estate of £1000 or nearly as much, over and above all legacies in his will. His widow Joan was his executrix, and his four daughters (one now deceased) were left in her charge. Edward Nethersole, who had a competent estate in lands, though encumbered by debts, became a suitor to Joan. A contract of marriage was agreed, whereby Nethersole was to bind himself to give £100 to each of the four daughters at the age of eighteen or on marriage, over and above any legacies from Richard Hooker, if he had no issue by Joan. He therefore entered into bonds to John and Robert Churchman in £1200. The marriage then took place, and Nethersole thus became seized of Hooker's estate, to the amount of £800 or more. He thus was able to discharge his lands in Kent of their encumbrances, and to buy more land to the annual value of £20.

Shortly after, Joan died, leaving no issue by Nethersole, who should thereupon have paid £300 to the three surviving daughters. But, seeking to evade his bond, he conveyed his lands to William Nutt and those in Canterbury to William Watmer for £770. No lands remained to secure the bond, and his son and heir Thomas was thus freed from this charge.

All lands outside Canterbury were conveyed in trust for Thomas, on condition that he confirmed the conveyance of the Canterbury lands to Watmer. This was done when Thomas came of age. He then received £400 still unpaid of the £770 and Watmer reconveyed to him the other lands, which Thomas therefore holds by purchase and not as heir of Edward. They are therefore not liable as security for the bond. The whole transaction was fraudulent, and has defrauded the daughters.

Nethersole died intestate. William Dalby, as administrator of his estate, is concealing its assets. The £400 received by Thomas for the lands should be part of the estate, and liable under the bond. Thomas Nethersole and Dalby are cited to answer.

signed *Ri: Lydall*

Answer of THOMAS NETHERSOLE, gentleman, sworn on
20 October 1610.

Edward Nethersole had a dowry of £700 with Joan Hooker.
On 12 March 1601, shortly before his marriage with her, he
entered into an indenture[1] with her father John Churchman and
her brother Robert, which is now in Thomas' possession. There
were then four daughters, to each of whom Richard Hooker had
left £100, which was put in trust with the two Churchmans by
Hooker's orders while still living. The Churchmans undertook
to Nethersole to use this £400 for the benefit of the daughters
and to pay each her portion at the age of eighteen or upon
marriage, with interest. Within two days of sealing this indenture
they were to enter into a bond of £600 to Nethersole to this
effect, and to free Nethersole of any liability in this respect.
Nethersole on his part undertook to leave them in possession of
the £400 for that purpose. He also undertook to maintain the
daughters up to the age of eighteen or until marriage, or for the
duration of his marriage to Joan. It was agreed that if Joan died
leaving no issue by Nethersole, he would pay any surviving
daughters £100 each at the age of eighteen or upon marriage,
in addition to Hooker's legacy of £100 each.

During his lifetime, Nethersole did in fact so maintain the
daughters at his own cost, as agreed. It seems to Thomas that
the £400 held in trust by the Churchmans must have been part
of the total dowry of £700, else why should Nethersole have
undertaken to assure possession to them? Thomas is not liable
for any part of the portions of the daughters. Hooker's legacy
is a matter solely for the Churchmans. The additional £100 each
was merely of Nethersole's good will, and Thomas is not bound
to pay it. Nethersole died intestate; Dalby is administrator;
Thomas, eldest son and heir, is not concerned; and no land held
in fee simple has come to him from his father.

The conveyance by Nethersole to Nutt of lands in the parish
of St Peter's, Canterbury, was *bona fide*. On 21 July 1607 a
conveyance was made for £770 to William Watmer, Alderman
of Canterbury, of a house occupied by him in St Peter's, Canterbury, also of a house, lands and pasture in Holy Cross, Canterbury,
by Nethersole and Thomas. On the same day a second similar

---

[1] This was the marriage-contract, the terms of which are now set forth.

conveyance was made of other houses and lands, including Nethersole's own residence

in Wincheape within the parishe of St Mildred or St Marye Castle within the Citye of Canterbury,

a house with barns in Wincheap called Stonehall, three acres of land called Batterdane in Thannington, Kent, a house with twenty acres in Whitstable, five houses in St Peter's, Canterbury, and two gardens with lodges in the same parish. This second conveyance provided that the properties concerned should be for the use of Nethersole during his life, thereafter to the use of Watmer, and after three years to be reconveyed to Thomas if Thomas confirmed the first conveyance.[1] These transactions have now been completed, since the death of Nethersole, and on 12 February 1610 Watmer has carried out the reconveyance provided for.

It was further provided, by an indenture of 23 July 1607, that Watmer should pay to Nethersole and his wife Joan £40 a year out of the lands concerned in the second conveyance, the price to be paid under which was £400 but was not in fact paid. Watmer, in fact, cleared himself of this indenture by a capital payment of £225.[2]

Further, Nethersole married Ellen, daughter of Thomas Stoughton, who was the mother of Thomas and died ten years before Nethersole. Her father by his will left to her and so to Thomas an inn called the Three Kings in All Saints', Canterbury, also a house called the Pied Bull with five other houses in St Mary Bredman, with a hop-garden in Wincheap and land in Thannington. These were the only properties held in fee simple by Thomas, who inherited none such from Nethersole, though Nethersole took the revenues from these properties inherited from Stoughton.

Answer of WILLIAM DALBY, sworn on 5 November 1610.

Dalby has administered Nethersole's estate properly, as set out in former Answers to Bills by Thomas in Michaelmas 1607 and

---

[1] Occupiers named are J. Hollier, Leon Ashenden, Alderman Thomas Halke, Richard Braricke, Thomas Clarke, Alderman Ralph Bawden.

[2] The transactions are clearly designed to evade the consequences of debt and forfeiture, for the benefit of Thomas.

by Edmund and Elizabeth Calton in Easter 1608. Dalby has long since ceased to be administrator of the estate, now administered by Elizabeth, daughter of Nethersole and wife of Edmund Calton. He understands that a debt of £400 due from Watmer was compounded by Thomas for £200 odd, which was paid. The Caltons are now suing Dalby in King's Bench, in contravention of a former order of Star Chamber, in respect of two bonds to Nethersole from Harlackenden and Wood for the payment of £40. Dalby is ready to surrender these on an order by the Court of Chancery.

signed Fr. Rodes.

(c)

Hooker v. Evans

Bill of ALICE, CICELY and MARGARET HOOKER, dated 13 April 1611.

Edward Nethersole, gentleman, deceased, late of Canterbury, married Joan the widow of Richard Hooker. Before or upon the marriage, Joan advanced £1000 to Nethersole, who entered into a covenant and bonds of £1200 to pay to each of the plaintiffs, and also to a fourth sister now deceased, £100 at the age of eighteen or upon marriage, if there were no issue of his marriage with Joan. Shortly after, Joan died, with no such issue.

But Nethersole's estate fell into decay and debt, with law-suits and other causes, and he was unable to pay these portions. He had a charge to pay £50 to a daughter of his own, upon a legacy left in trust with him by her grandfather, upon her marriage to Zachary Evans. He therefore bound himself to pay Evans an annuity of £5 on certain lands in Kent. Later on he was prepared to pay the £50 and wished to cancel the annuity. Evans persuaded him to let him receive the £50 and also the annuity, in order to defraud Nethersole's creditors. Nethersole died shortly after.

Evans thereupon demanded afresh the £50 from Nethersole's son Thomas, who paid it, being ignorant of the previous payment, and is therefore the less able to pay the Hookers their portions. Evans has, indeed, embezzled most of Nethersole's estate, under pretence of deeds of gift to his daughter Elizabeth, to his daughter Jane (Mrs Evans), worth £40; and Elizabeth gave to him a carpet and coverlet worth £30. There is no executor or administrator to proceed against at Common Law. Of the £300 due, £200 has been due and payable these three years.[1]

Now Thomas Nethersole has compounded with the Hookers to pay them £200 at the end of five years more, in 1616, or £150 in all if he pays now. They have therefore lost by their forbearance for three years. Thomas agrees that they may recover if they can at law from Zachary Evans, against whom they now are proceeding.

Answer of ZACHARY EVANS, sworn on 23 April 1611.

There is already a similar suit pending by the Hookers against Evans, to the same purpose, which has proceeded to depositions and is yet undetermined.

The Bill is unprecise, not naming the plaintiffs fully, and there is in fact an administrator (named in the former Bill).

The facts are that when Nethersole married Mrs Hooker her dowry was only £600–700, not £1000, and she had wasted £100 of this dowry during her widowhood. Nethersole's covenant and bond are admitted. Nothing was due to the Hookers before his death, when none of them was eighteen years of age or married. The repayment of the £50 by Edward Nethersole is denied. Thomas repaid Evans the £50, plus £7 to £10 arrears due, to cancel the annuity, which was done. Evans has only had further goods worth £10 plus various trifles. He has been at great charge for Nethersole, and yet his widow keeps a cupboard with drawers worth 13s. 4d.[2] His daughter Elizabeth, who married Edmund Calton, gave Evans a carpet and coverlet worth £4, but this was during Nethersole's lifetime; and the Caltons owe more to Evans.

Depositions[3]

13 February 1610. ORWIN HUGHES, Clerk, Vicar of Kingston-on-Thames, Surrey, aged 34, knew Nethersole for 4–5 years before his death. Hughes and Evans borrowed £20 for him

[1] Alice reached the age of eighteen on 10 May 1608, Cicely on 21 April 1609. Margaret must have been born after 13 April 1593.

[2] Nethersole married a third wife (Joan, cf. p. 163) after Mrs Hooker's death. His first wife was Ellen, daughter of Thomas Stoughton or Stocton.

[3] These depositions, from C. 24/362/44, pertain to the previous suit referred to in Evans' *Answer*, as appears from their dates.

from John Cloke, and Nethersole gave them security, a bond of £20 from Walter Harlackenden and a deed of gift of goods worth more than £20, which Evans now has in his possession, though Nethersole wished Hughes to have them in keeping. Evans was willing to pay a proper price to the estate for the goods, and Hughes agreed to write to John Huntley[1] to seek agreement rather than go to law.

(signs) *per me Ow. Hughes:*

16 February 1610. THOMAS NETHERSOLE, gentleman, of the City of Canterbury, aged 22, knew of a deed of sale whereby his father made over brass and pewter vessels and other household goods to Hughes and Evans. It was either in respect of a loan of £20, or of £250 left in trust with Nethersole, to be given to his two daughters, under the will of their grandfather Stocten (or Stoughton). He does not think the deed was fraudulent. Within half a year after Nethersole's death, Thomas paid over to Mrs Evans her portion of £50 from her grandfather. He had heard his father say he had promised Evans a further £50 with her, but Thomas did not pay this further sum. Evans and Hughes were paid £20 on Nethersole's bond, by Harlackenden. Evans, it seems, took away from Nethersole's house 'a whole chest of armour', by force or pretending a deed, worth £4-5. Nethersole said that Evans was to assure to his wife a jointure of £15 per annum before he was to come into possession of her portion. An offer was made of £6-7 for a great pair of andirons, but Thomas does not know what was offered for the arras coverlet and carpet.

(signs) *Thomas Nethersoll*

20 February 1611. WILLIAM DALBY, Citizen and Merchant Tailor of London, aged 47.

Evans took away from Nethersole's house goods worth £80. His only excuse was his loan of £20, which had been repaid by Harlackenden. Dalby has heard of a deed of gift made by Nethersole to Evans and to Elizabeth Calton, before his marriage with Hooker's widow. This was done with the purpose of defrauding the Hooker girls or to deceive their mother. The chest of armour was not included in the deed. And a jointure of £15 per annum was covenanted for.

(signs) *Wm Daulby*

[1] Acting here as elsewhere for the Hookers.

25 February 1611. EDWARD WEAVER, gentleman, of St Gregories in Paul's, London, aged 24, formerly served and attended on Nethersole. About the end of Easter Term, four years ago come Easter (i.e. in Easter 1607), Nethersole was committed to the Fleet on a censure of the Star Chamber. While he was in prison, Zachary Evans, Clerk, his son-in-law, came to see him, pretending charity, love and duty, and desire to comfort him and relieve his needs. Nethersole asked him for money; Evans said he would try; but came back to the Fleet saying that none was to be had in London, but that he had a friend who would lend on a bond by Evans and his friend Hughes if Nethersole would make a Bill of Sale of his goods in their favour. Nethersole did so. Weaver has seen the deed, signed and sealed by Nethersole, and bearing the date 11 May 1607. It is the deed now shown to Weaver in Court, and it grants to Evans and Hughes, as security for a loan of £20,

1 pair latten Andirons	1 copper Cauldron
1 pair small Andirons, 'serving in the stead of Crepers'	1 green cushion chair
	2 rushen embroidered stools
All pewter stamped with Nethersole's arms	4 window cushions
	1 gold ring
2 brazen Cauldrons	3 links

These goods were worth £40 and more, and it was agreed that they were not to be dealt with by Evans and Hughes unless the £20 loan was unpaid, except that Hughes was to have the ring only in any case; and on these conditions Nethersole signed the deed.

Weaver has heard Nethersole say that he made a deed of gift to his own two daughters—the intent being to defraud Mrs Hooker—because he had not received with Mrs Hooker the full dowry he anticipated. Long before his death Nethersole said that he had paid Evans the full portion of Jane, Evans' wife, bequeathed to her by her grandfather. He often said that he had promised Evans to give Jane another £50 to add to her grandfather's £50; Thomas and others said this also was paid to Evans and Thomas had his receipt for it. Weaver has seen an Answer made in Chancery by Richard Wood of Hollingbourne, Kent, stating that Wood paid Evans £20 to discharge Nethersole's debt of £20. Evans was never sued for his bond, nor paid any part of the £20 debt himself. The Bill of Sale was therefore void.

Evans took advantage of Nethersole's deed of gift to his two daughters, Jane and Elizabeth, to take out of Nethersole's house the following:

8 Needlework cushions	1 graven corselet	1 leading staff
1 old carpet	2 white corselets furnished	1 chest for armour
2 brass pots	1 musket with rest	4 old daggers
1 brass skimmer	1 fowling piece	1 old sword
9 Candlesticks	1 caliver	3 Spanish pikes
42 lbs. of pewter	2 swords and daggers	1 cupboard with drawers
1 brazen ladle	1 graven target with gauntlet	2 old chests
1 long arras carpet		1 bill
1 arras coverlet		

worth in all about £30.

Weaver has heard Evans admit that he should have made his wife a jointure of £50 per annum before he got Nethersole's promised £50; but he never did so. An offer of £10 was made for the great andirons. Weaver recognizes the two documents now shown to him, being a Deed of Gift and a Power of Attorney, both dated 11 May 1607 and signed by Nethersole and witnessed by Weaver.

(signs) *Edward Weaver*

30 April 1611. EDMUND CALTON, gentleman, of St Clement Danes, London, aged 46, knows of the Bill of Sale of goods worth 40 marks to £30, as security for a bond of £20, and the note of its contents, including a great pair of brass andirons with 'crepers', fire shovels and tongs, twelve garnishes of pewter, *etc.* The bond of £20 by Harlackenden and Wood was also assigned to Evans and Hughes, and was paid up by Wood to them.

Calton is the administrator of Nethersole's estate. Evans admitted to him receipt of the £20 from Wood, but Calton could never recover the goods taken away by Evans, though he would have been content with half of them.

Nethersole's deed of gift to Evans and Elizabeth (Calton's late wife), of which Calton has a copy, was not fraudulent but was intended to ensure a conscionable legacy to Elizabeth from her grandfather Stoughton (or Stockton) in Nethersole's trust. Jane's portion of £50 was paid to Evans by Nethersole or soon after her death. Evans' claim for £7 interest is unjustified. The annuity of £5 granted by Nethersole was only as security for the legacies.

Evans took advantage of the deed of gift to take away goods not sanctioned by Nethersole, who left Elizabeth in charge of his goods and gave her the keys 'of his linen and household stuff in his house at Canterbury while he was in prison in the Fleet. But Evans, in collusion with his mother-in-law Mrs Nethersole, came to Elizabeth saying that Nethersole had been sentenced in Star Chamber to forfeit all his goods to the King; it would therefore be better to let Evans take them away and save them. Elizabeth refused, as being put in trust by her father; and Evans threatened to burn the deed of gift before her face. Elizabeth often before her death reproached him with all this, and told Calton how

when my brother Evans dyd see I would not yeeld to let him have the keyes because of the Charge my father gave me to loke to the goods he then thretened that he would burne the...dede of guifte before my face and would allso be a wytnes againste me for the rest of my porcon then resting in anothers hands and quoth shee at the last what throughe the...thretinge of Evans and the perswasion of my mother and some others I threwe downe the keyes amonge them and went awaye weping.

So Evans took away a cartload of goods, worth £30, to his house, and after Nethersole's death he took also a chest of armour with

1 graven corselet or 'curet' of proof furnished with gauntlets and head-piece
2 white corselets or 'curets', furnished, for pikemen
1 musket with bandoleers ('bandalers')
1 caliver with flash and touchbox, etc.
1 old bible, with divers other books and chronicles
1 cupboard or 'cabonet', etc.

being another £5 worth.

Moreover, Evans himself said that Audrey Nicolls of Canterbury paid him 20 nobles (£6. 13s. 4d.) for the andirons with other andirons, shovel, etc. in part exchange. Mrs Nethersole and others have affirmed that offers of £10 were made at Canterbury and refused by Evans.

The deed of gift in parchment is dated 18 January 45 Elizabeth, and the paper bill of sale is dated 11 May 5 James I, both now shown.

signed *Edm: Calton*

Reports and Certificates, by the MASTERS IN CHANCERY.

Report, dated 13 January 1613.

$$\left.\begin{array}{l}\text{Alice}\\\text{Cicely}\\\text{Margaret}\end{array}\right\}\begin{array}{l}\text{Hooker}\\\text{plaintiffs}\end{array}\ v.\left\{\begin{array}{l}\text{Zachary Evans}\\\text{Richard Wood}\\\text{Wm Dalby}\end{array}\right.\quad\text{defendants}[1]$$

In pursuance of an order of the Court dated 25 November 1612, the parties were called and the pleadings examined. Edward Nethersole, it appears, should have paid to the three plaintiffs £300, £100 each. After a suit in Chancery between the plaintiffs and Thomas Nethersole, heir of Edward, in view of the decayed estate of Thomas, a compromise was arrived at for a payment of £200, with his agreement.

Zachary Evans admits that of Nethersole's goods which came into his possession, £29 worth might be claimed by the plaintiffs, but Nethersole owed him £12.

Richard Wood and Walter Harlackenden entered into several bonds on behalf of Nethersole. £5 was paid by Wood to the late Edward Calton and his wife Elizabeth, administratrix of Nethersole. But debts due to Nethersole, e.g. by Wood, complicate accounts.

It is ordered that (1) Evans is to pay to the plaintiffs £12 out of the £29 worth of goods in two payments of £6, on May Day next and Michaelmas following; payment to be made in the market-place at Kingston, (2) Evans is to deliver at once to them two sets of armour with gauntlets, to be chosen by them out of the three taken by him, (3) Evans is then to be cleared of all responsibility in Nethersole's estate, and Wood and Harlackenden are discharged of their bonds, (4) Wood is to pay the plaintiffs £35 on 28 February next, in the Chapel of the Rolls.

signed *Jo Benet.*

[1] Dalby was entered as defendant apparently because he was for a time administrator of Nethersole's estate, Nethersole dying intestate. He appears as a witness. Nor is Wood cited as defendant in the Bill, which cites only Evans. But evidently there was a multiplicity of suits arising out of the Hookers' claims upon Nethersole's estate. Dalby was a friend of Mrs Hooker who conducted the marriage negotiations with Nethersole.

(d)

Hooker v. Huntley

Bill of ALICE HOOKER, dated 30 April 1623.

Alice Hooker is one of the daughters of Richard Hooker, late Doctor of Divinity and Master of the Temple, who at his death left £400 for them with John Churchman. John and Robert Churchman bound themselves in £800 to their trustees under the will, John Spencer and Anthony Stratford. John Churchman fell into decay and handed over to Robert goods to pay the legacy. Robert admitted responsibility for £400, alleging that he paid up £100 to Stratford, leaving £300 due. Stratford died, leaving Richard Stratford liable as his executor. Robert was ready to pay £300 in return for discharge from his bond.

In 1609–10 the daughters, through John Huntley, M.A. of St John's College, Oxford, their guardian, sued Robert and Stratford in Chancery. The Lord Chancellor decreed on 1 March 1610 that Robert should pay £300, and Stratford £140 (including £40 interest), to Francis Evington in trust for the daughters. So £440 was paid for the benefit of the sisters. Alice's share, £146. 13s. 4d., was deposited in trust with Huntley as guardian. Now Huntley retains this for his own use, being Alice's whole fortune. He alleges that she is contracted in marriage and therefore he is keeping it safe for her. This is however untrue. Huntley has given no bond or security for the money.

signed *R. Heath*.

Answer of JOHN HUNTLEY, sworn on 13 May 1623.

The facts are as stated, up to the payment of £440 deposited with Huntley as guardian. But the whole sum was not received until two years after the Chancery decree. After Hooker's death the daughters were left in fact without means, therefore Huntley, being of kin to them, out of charity to them undertook their cause at law against Churchman and Stratford, thereby losing much money and time, and to the hindrance of his studies. This and other suits on their behalf had cost him £50 at least in money alone.

About five years ago Alice Hooker, being then over 21 years of age, and Thomas Langley, Stationer, of St Sepulchre's, London, were contracted to marry, before witnesses. Therefore Huntley soon after the betrothal paid over to Langley £150 as Alice's portion, and holds Langley's receipt for this. There was no fraud in this transaction.[1]

Huntley has maintained, or paid for the maintenance, of three of the sisters for some six or seven years, spending money for their education, maintenance and apparelling, to the value of £100 at least. All these expenses on their behalf have in fact obliged Huntley to borrow money at interest to meet them.

signed Jo: Martin.

(e)

Huntley v. Huntley, Hooker et al.

Bill of JOHN HUNTLEY of Chipstead, Surrey, gentleman, dated 22 April 1624.

On 30 April 1623 Alice Hooker cited Huntley in Chancery in respect of £150 said to be due to her. Huntley answered claiming a reduction of the amount for expenses. He is still anxious to pay what is rightly due, out of goodwill to her 'and the reverence he had unto her deceased father'.

Huntley owns in fee simple the messuage Deane House with barns, gardens and lands called Grovefield[2] in the parishes of Chipstead and Gatton, now occupied by the Rev. Edward Shove, George Pope and Daniel Best. On 29 May 1623, Huntley with the consent of his brother Edward Huntley entered into a statute staple to Thomas Wood of Croydon for £300, for the use and benefit of Alice Hooker and her heirs, to be cancelled upon payment by Huntley to Wood on 20 November 1623 for the benefit of Alice, 'at the Fount stone in the Temple Church London'. Huntley intended to sell lands to raise the necessary money, as he told Wood, Alice and Edward.

---

[1] Certainly Alice did not in fact marry Langley. The argument seems to be that she is still contracted to him. But it is incredible that Langley could keep her dowry in such circumstances. Indeed, Huntley abandoned this position in his counter-suit next year: cf. Appendix C, II, ii (e) below. It seems as if the quarrel must have been patched up somehow, for Alice Hooker died, at Chipstead (Huntley's home), in 1649, still unmarried.

[2] 'and Gatton Longfeilde' *deleted*.

About Midsummer 1623, Huntley agreed with Shove to sell to him 40 acres for £280. Shove agreed, after inspection of title, and later refused to complete, alleging defective title. Now the defendants have in their hands the deeds of his land and the defeazance of his bond, and are impeding any possible sale by Huntley, so that he cannot raise the £150 for Wood. They intend to prosecute Huntley on his bond at Common Law.

Huntley cites Edward Huntley, Alice Hooker, Edward Shove and Thomas Wood.

signed Jo: Martin.

Answer of EDWARD HUNTLEY and ALICE HOOKER, sworn on 29 April 1624.

No money was spent by John Huntley in securing Alice's legacy. Ellen Huntley, mother of John, spent £80 in recovering the portions due to Alice and her sisters: no one else spent money to this end. If John spent any, it was certainly less than the interest due on Alice's portion, detained by him for over thirteen years.

John has in fact paid to Alice only forty shillings on one occasion. He has no good will to her, as is evident from his suing her in Chancery. He could not indeed without disgrace conduct such a suit, and this was the reason why Edward agreed to let him make the bond of 29 May 1623 to Wood for the benefit of Alice.

Shove and William Smith of London, mercer, went to Edward's house and told him of the agreement to sell 40 acres. Shove needed money to complete the purchase, so Edward offered to lend him money at 8 % or 9 % interest, and is still ready to do so, to get the matter settled. He cannot say whether Shove is still agreed to buy.

Edward and Alice have not in any way decried John's title to sell, nor do they hold any document of his.

signed Ro Heath.

iii. The Bankruptcy of John Churchman

Abstract of Proceedings in Churchman *v.* Bradshaw *et al.*
Star Chamber 8. 98/12

Churchman *v.* Bradshaw *et al.*

Robert Churchman,
plaintiff, *v.*

⎧ Peter Bradshaw
⎪ Godfrey Bradshaw
⎨ Francis Bradshaw
⎪ Andrew Osborne
⎩ John Woodward, *et al.*, defendants

Robert Churchman of Enfield, gentleman, is suing the defendants for riotous entry upon his house at Enfield, and for assault.

i. *Bill* of ROBERT CHURCHMAN. 30 January 1606.

In February 1597, upon the conclusion of a marriage-contract between Robert Churchman and Anne, daughter of Richard Benyan of Coxhall, John Churchman agreed to assure to Anne as jointure a house and lands, to the value of £40 a year, while Benyan agreed to give her a dowry of £500. On 7 February, John Churchman entered into bonds to Benyan for £600, undertaking to leave to Robert and his heirs, after his own death and that of his wife, a half part of all his lands and also of all his other property, on an equality with his eldest son John the younger, with the possibility of an earlier settlement. On these undertakings, Benyan paid over the dowry and the marriage took place.

On 23 May 1604, John Churchman duly conveyed to Robert, *bona fide* and not in trust, a house and lands in Enfield and Edmonton, by deed enrolled, and his bond of £600 was cancelled.

Almost a year later, in February 1605, a petition in bankruptcy against John Churchman was made to the Lord Chancellor, Ellesmere, by Peter Bradshaw, Godfrey Bradshaw, Andrew Osborne, Alexander Ashurst, and John Langley, for their own ends and injuriously to Churchman. On 25 February a Commission was set up of six men, of whom four were to be a quorum, and one of the quorum was to be either Nicholas Fuller or Nicholas Collyn.

On 30 February (*sic*) Peter Bradshaw with the other defendants approached Fuller and Collyn corruptly, to further their own claims, offering bribes of £20 to each, which were accepted, with a view to especial favour in the conduct of the Commission. Fuller and Collyn delivered signed and sealed blank warrants to the defendants to call such witnesses at the hearing as they desired. The Commission met under these conditions, declared Churchman bankrupt, and also declared that his conveyance of house and lands to Robert was made on trust and after his bankruptcy. And this although Robert has been seized of the house and has lived there for the last six years.

Finally, while Robert was at his house at Enfield with his family, on 8 June 1605, the defendants assembled there with other persons, twenty in all, being armed, assaulted Robert and forcibly and riotously entered his house. Robert, seeking to save himself, ran to a room in his house which was secure, thus escaping their fury. But his wife Anne, and a certain Mrs Mary Cutts,[1] both being great with child, were in terror, became ill from shock and were in danger of death as a result of this riot.

ii. (*a*) *Answer* of NICHOLAS COLLYN, sworn on 22 February 1606.

The Bill is mendacious in its accusations of bribery, favour to creditors, and blank warrants. The Commissioners did not neglect to call witnesses to prove that the conveyance was *bona fide*. Collyn gave much time to the Commission, some whole days and many afternoons, to his great loss by neglect of his clients. All he had for his pains was a free-will gift from the creditors, a total of thirty to forty shillings.

(*b*) *Answer* of NICHOLAS FULLER, sworn on 2 July 1606.

The suit is merely vexatious. Robert Churchman has got into his hands a great part of the assets of his bankrupt father. The bankruptcy is clear, on the petition and the evidence of creditors who are his loving neighbours and friends, and who have been deceitfully used. John Churchman himself has expressed his shame. Some of his creditors were bound for him in great sums, yet offered further credit and support even 'when he began to

---

[1] This was Robert's sister Mary. See ii (*c*) below.

keep his house'. John himself behaved ill, in paying off some great creditors in full before the due date, while neglecting his own loving neighbours who have not received the half of their claims, and leaving nothing unconveyed or unencumbered.

The Commissioners found John's debts to amount to £4000, with unencumbered assets hardly amounting to £100 to meet them. They therefore made enquiry, at the request of the creditors, especially with recent conveyances. So hearing counsel on both sides, and consulting with Sir Edmund Anderson, Chief Justice of the Common Pleas, Sir Thomas Walmesley, Justice of the Common Pleas, and Sir Edward Cooke, Attorney General, they made orders according to the opinion of Sir Edward Cooke, and made the property in question available for the creditors. This was all dealt with by Fuller, with due care.

It was better policy to make these assets available. For, if the decision was erroneous, Robert had a remedy at law. But if the Commission had not decided as it did, the creditors had no remedy at law. Therefore, despite doubt in certain instances, Fuller favoured the creditors. Had he been Robert's best friend in London, he could not have done otherwise.

Fuller took no fee in his capacity as Commissioner for all his labour and his loss of practice and fees as lawyer; whatever he received from the creditors he returned despite their protests. However, it is true that he received fees from them, which he retained, for his legal advice to them and for his labours in conveyancing, penning, visiting the Attorney General, etc., being in all some £4, whereas his time thus engaged was truly worth more than £12.

The actual conveyance of the property in question was not performed by John Churchman until some six or seven years after Robert's marriage, and until John was on the verge of bankruptcy. Moreover, John had already, it is reported, conveyed to Robert his valuable London house; the Commissioners therefore made the Enfield property available for the creditors.

As for the blank warrants, it might be argued that they *were* blank warrants.

(c) *Answer* of the CREDITORS, sworn on 27 February 1606.

The suit is malicious. Robert Churchman has used devices to obtain protection for himself against the creditors in their action at Common Law. He 'termeth himself a gentleman beinge late

Citizen and merchantaylor of London usinge the trade of a draper with his father'. And he is merely trying to force a favourable composition.

It is true that the conveyance to Robert was made as stated in May 2 James I. But long before this John and Robert lived in Watling Street among their neighbours the present creditors Andrew Osborne, Godfrey Bradshaw and Peter Bradshaw. John had for many years been a draper, in such high repute and credit among his neighbours that he had twice been Warden of his Company, and once Master; also he had been chosen by the vote of the citizens to be Chamberlain of London, an office of great credit and trust. The defendants, having the highest respect for John,

did vse him as their father or brother...some of them calling him father and being redy as his Children & dere frends to travell for him and to become bounden for him as his suerties...without expecting any recompense.

In January 1605, John began to 'keep his howse', to avoid his creditors, to the damage of his credit. Some of the defendants thereupon offered to enter upon further bonds of surety for him. But John used them unkindly and dishonestly, by not repaying them, and plotted with Robert to convey all his assets to his sons Robert and John, and to his son-in-law Robert Cutt. To meet his debts of £4000, he left free assets amounting only to £40. Therefore they petitioned for a Commission in bankruptcy.

On 4 February 1605, the examination took place of John, Robert, and other witnesses. It appeared that John conveyed the Enfield property to Robert within a year before his bankruptcy. Also, as we have heard, there was a conveyance of his house and shop in London, which was sold (so we hear) by John and Robert to Sir Roger Jones, Knight and Alderman, for £700, being a full half of John's landed property; and this within two months before his bankruptcy.

The £700 thus obtained went to meet a debt of £600 to Sir William Craven, two months before it was due, and another of £200 to Randolph Manning, skinner, four months before it was due. These two are wealthy men, while we, who are John's neighbours, and poor, cannot even obtain ten shillings in the pound of our claims.

Again, two months before his bankruptcy, John gave to Robert an irrevocable power of attorney to recover all debts due to John, of the value of £4000. The best of these debts were transferred by Robert to himself. He cancelled many debts and bills due to John in Ireland, conveyed some to John Churchman the younger and to Robert Cutt, and cancelled and defaced debts in John's ledgers amounting to £800.

As for the accusation of bribery, the creditors had thirty interviews with Nicholas Fuller, who also went twelve times on their business to the Guildhall. For all this he was only paid a fee of £4, when his time was worth £8.[1]

The warrants were, in fact, issued to them blank, for they were not at the time quite sure of the names of the witnesses they wished to be heard.

As for the riot alleged, it is true that they were at Enfield on the occasion stated, in order to see a lease sealed, to have it tried by *ejectione firme*. At the same time Robert was arrested by the sheriff's officer, on a *latitat* of Middlesex. Robert attempted to make a *rescous*, and offered to strike the bailiff, whereupon Godfrey Bradshaw drew his sword to protect the bailiff and Robert then ran away. No hurt was done to anyone, and there were no weapons save this one sword.

Finally, Robert Churchman is a villain who will spend all he has to prevent the creditors getting their just dues. His father John, being well aware of the losses he had brought upon his honest and loving neighbours, said to Peter Bradshaw

that he was ashamed to looke any honest man on the face because he had delt soe badlie and dishonestlie wth his lovinge neighbo^rs, and wished that there were a lawe to take awaye his life for deallinge soe vnhonestlye, and wished that he might be layed in some darke dungeon where he might never see honest man againe in the face.

iii. *Replication* of ROBERT CHURCHMAN, sworn on Tuesday, 25 November 1606.

The statements made in the Bill are all maintained as true. Bribes were in fact given and taken; if returned, they were returned after this suit in Star Chamber was begun.

---

[1] Fuller himself, we observe, valued his own time more highly than did his creditors even when they might be stretching a point in their own interests, as here. For his connection with anti-Church books, see Star Chamber 8. 19/7.

The conveyance of the Enfield property is good in law, being made long before the bankruptcy. It could never have been attached for the benefit of the creditors, had it not been for a dishonest Commission, in especial Nicholas Fuller.

The assets available, in goods and book-debts, if properly managed and disposed of, are sufficient to meet the creditors.

As for the house in London, it was conveyed to Robert, not in pursuance of John's bond to Benyan, but as security to Robert in respect of various sums of money procured by him for John after the marriage. These debts, incurred by Robert for John, were met by the sale of the house. Every other plea by the defendants in their Answers is traversed and denied.

iv. *Depositions* by DEFENDANTS.

(*a*) WILLIAM WOOD, a Serjeant at Mace, aged 35, examined on 28 January, 1608.

Some time in May, June and July last, in 1607, at the request of Peter Bradshaw, he arrested Robert Churchman. Bradshaw promised him forty shillings for so doing, but in fact neither Bradshaw nor anyone else paid him.

(*b*) JOHN WOODWARD, Scrivener.

Was Clerk to the Commissioners in Bankruptcy upon John Churchman, and was paid £7 for his labours.

iv. Nethersole in Star Chamber

Abstract of Proceedings in Nethersole *v.* Chamberlaine
Star Chamber 8. 220/27

Nethersole *v.* Chamberlaine

Bill of EDWARD NETHERSOLE, dated 13 November 1606.

The Bill, which is long, prolix and confused, rehearses antecedent proceedings in Star Chamber and at Common Law, arising out of the disposal of the estate of Francis Pettifer of Southampton, mariner, who died in 1598 or 1599. The suit is apparently a counter-suit to one begun in Easter Term of the same year 1606 by Ralph Robins of Milbroke, Hants. yeoman, the surviving executor of the estate, the other, Robert Foell, gentleman, being deceased.

Robins *v.* Nethersole. Star Chamber.

Pettifer *v.*
Robins.
Court of
Common
Pleas.

After the death of Francis Pettifer, two of his relatives, Nicholas Pettifer, clerk in Holy Orders, and his son Nicholas the younger, of Canterbury, propounded a bond of £200 for a debt of £100 made by Francis to Nicholas the elder, his 'father-in-law',[1] and dated 20 October 1595. This was resisted by the executors. The Pettifers took them to the Common Law, where the executors were not able to support by evidence their allegation that the bond was a forgery. It was upheld. The executors apparently had already distributed the estate to the legatees. And Ralph Robins was kept in prison for over six months until he was able to make the necessary payment to discharge the bond.

Robins *v.*
Pettifer.
Star
Chamber.

Subsequently, Robins' enquiries brought to light the material for a more precise formulation of the charge that the bond was forged, and he took proceedings in Star Chamber against the two Pettifers of Canterbury and also against Edward Turfett, schoolmaster, of the same city. It was alleged that the true date of the making of the bond was early in November 1598, after the death of Francis Pettifer. It was forged, in the intent to deprive the legatees under the will of the testator. The charge was that the Pettifers and Turfett forged the bond, gave it a false date, forged signatures and seals, and suborned three witnesses, John Bucke, Isaac Obaston, and Robert Pillinge, to add their names. They subsequently added a fourth name, that of Peter Griggs, mariner, said to have been a witness to the bond and actually the writer of the bond. There was never, in fact, any such person as Peter Griggs, and the intent was to make impossible the discovery of the forgery.

Nicholas Pettifer was convicted of forgery by the Court and was condemned to pay double damages and costs to Ralph Robins, that is, £400 damages and £80 costs.

Among other witnesses appearing at the hearing of the suit were George Pettifer, another son of Nicholas, and Edward Nethersole, who gave evidence in support of the bond. Nicholas Pettifer the younger could not be served with a *sub-poena* to appear for examination, as he was in a far country, having been conveyed away to escape examination.

[1] The phrase can mean 'father-in-law' or 'step-father'. Francis Pettifer was unmarried. Could his mother have married another Pettifer before marrying Nicholas? I see no other explanation.

On 11 May 1601, Edward Nethersole testified in reply to the 4th and 5th Interrogatories put to him as follows: In October five years ago, he was in the house of Nicholas Pettifer in Canterbury, when Francis Pettifer, in his presence and in the presence of Nicholas, signed, sealed and delivered the bond; and he heard the bond read over on delivery. He was not asked to sign as a witness, but he was there, as was George Pettifer, and also Peter Griggs who read the bond over. He also recalled the dress worn by Francis on the occasion. George Pettifer was similarly examined on oath on the same day.

All this evidence, Robins' Bill stated, was untrue and was perjured. But Nethersole in his Answer has denied this. Evidence has been taken on Commission. And the hearing of the case in Star Chamber is now fixed for a certain day.

Nethersole *v.* Chamberlaine. *Star Chamber.*

Nethersole is now, in this counter-suit, charging Robins' attorney at the Court of Common Pleas, Brian Chamberlaine of Hampshire, with corruptly maintaining and sustaining action on the part of Ralph Robins, to Nethersole's damage, from the Michaelmas Term of 1605 to the Michaelmas Term of 1606.

Demurrer of BRIAN CHAMBERLAINE, entered on Tuesday 25 November 1606.

The defendant demurs in law against this long and tedious Bill in 24 sheets. The charges are uncertain, and it is not stated in what ways he has been guilty of maintenance.[1]

Verdict and *Sentence* in ROBINS *v.* NETHERSOLE.

From c. 24/362/44. See App. C. II. ii (*c*) above.

Edward Nethersole was committed to the Fleet Prison, on a censure from the Court of Star Chamber in Easter Term 1607 (evidence of Edward Weaver). Sentence was given against him, and it was ordered that all his goods were to be forfeited to the King (evidence of Edmund Calton).[2]

[1] There can be no doubt that this Demurrer was accepted by the Court, and that it closed the proceedings in Nethersole's counter-suit.

[2] Weaver had been Nethersole's 'servant', and Calton was Nethersole's son-in-law. Their evidence is decisive.

III. *LETTER FROM ARCHBISHOP WHITGIFT*

The following letter, in the archives of the Dean and Chapter of Canterbury (MS Y. 14. 1), is transcribed from a photograph kindly communicated by Canon John Shirley, Headmaster of the King's School. The signature only is autograph.

Salutem in Chrõ. Whereas this bearer Mr Raven is coffended vnto me for a verie good scholler beinge an auncient M^r of Artes and one that throughe some longe cõtinuance and practise in keepinge a scholle at Wrotham in Kent is thought to be skillfull in teaching and bringinge vp of yo^wthe: These are to move yo^w in his behalfe and hartelie to praye yo^w, that if vpon yor owne triall yo^w shall finde him sufficient for yor purpose and aun-swerable to that reporte wch is given of him; then yo^w would be pleased the rather for my sake to shewe him favo^r and to admitt him for yor Scholl-maister in Canterburie. And so w^t my hartie coffendacõns I cõmitt yo^w to the tuicon of allmightie God. ffrom Croydon the xvth of September 1591.

yor assured Lovinge frend

Jo: Cantuar.

Appendix D

NOTES

I. THE AGE OF JOHN CHURCHMAN

John Churchman stated on 7 July 1613 that he was then ninety years of age (Appendix C above, p. 130). But I have found an earlier deposition made by him in Chancery, on 9 March 1594, when he gave his age as sixty (P.R.O. C 24/237/58). If we are to accept the former of these statements, he would have been born between 8 July 1522 and 7 July 1523; if the latter, between 10 March 1533 and 9 March 1534. There is thus a margin of error of ten years between these two estimates of his age by Churchman. I have, however, frequently observed a tendency among the aged in Elizabethan days, and indeed occasionally among their living successors, to magnify their feat of longevity. There were, for instance, more frequent claims to the age of one hundred years than one would expect. Once there was a true claim to the veneration accorded to advanced old age, there was a temptation to heighten that claim. And memory was less secure.

On the other hand, it may be urged, at an earlier period of elderliness, when still in full activity, there may be a temptation to diminish the tale of years. Shakespeare's Falstaff, for instance, though his white hairs witness against him, rebels against old age, and claims to be old only in judgment and understanding, otherwise in the vaward of his youth. And he assesses his age as 'some fifty or, by'r Lady, inclining to threescore'. He was not yet, in truth, 'blasted with antiquity', and was not resigned to the more venerable estate.

I cannot, however, produce any parallel to Falstaff in this respect among Elizabethan men with a more documentary authenticity. Sixty was, after all, an age which invited neither reticence nor exaggeration, and was an eminently right age for a man who in three months' time was to be elected Master of the Merchant Taylors' Company. I see no reason for suspecting that either a defective memory or innocent vanity intervened between the Court and the truth in Churchman's earlier deposition in 1594. I have therefore accepted this evidence that he was born in

1533/4. This would make him at most thirty-five when his son Robert was born, forty-eight when his youngest daughter Sara was born, fifty-five when his daughter Joan married Hooker, and eighty-four when he died. There is no record of his apprenticeship, but he was elected to the livery on 3 April 1570 and to the Court on 28 August 1582. His sons John and Robert became Free of the Company by Patrimony on 20 January 1583 and 9 August 1591 respectively.[1]

II. PRINTING BY LETTERS PATENT TO AUTHORS

The Stationers' Company had more serious problems to face than such private ventures as that of Sandys, who proceeded in faith without any protection or authority. The prerogative of the Crown, exercised since the beginnings of printing in England, opposed itself by occasional intervention to such a principle as they sought to lay down and to enforce. Against the weapon of a Letter Patent they had no remedy. And Letters Patent were not infrequently granted both by Elizabeth and by James, not only for books or classes of books, as is well known, but also even to authors desirous of printing and publishing works for their own profit, in order that they might have the due reward for their labours. This type of individual copyright obviously needed the co-operation of printers and booksellers, which does not seem to have been an obstacle, whatever the official views of the Company. There was an interesting Chancery suit in 1630, in which the Stationers' Company sought redress in respect of Letters Patent granted to Roger Wood and Simcock on 20 August 1628 for the printing of 'all breefes portraictures pictures Ballards damaske paper' etc., all such as 'may be conteyned vpon the one side of paper' (P.R.O. C 24/561/118). The printer John Haviland, in setting forth the abuse of Letters Patent in general, referred in his evidence to specific examples of grants 'to the authors themselves', evidently looked upon as extreme cases. Mr John Minsheu, he recalled, 'had a patent of priviledge...for the printing of his dictionary of dyvers Languages'. 'George Withers' had Letters Patent from James I 'for his owne hymnes

[1] Mr R. A. Smith, M.A., kindly informs me that the name of John Churchman does not appear among the names of City Chamberlains from 1563 to 1643, of which a list was printed by Mr A. B. Beavan in the *City Press*, 15 November 1902. I can only suggest that Churchman acted as a Deputy for the Chamberlain at some time.

or spiritual songes. And Mr Geo: Sandyes for his owne Workes.'
Mr Haviland might have added other examples, e.g. the grant to
Timothy Bright for his *Abridgement of the Book of Martyrs*, which
led to much trouble. I imagine that George Sandys' *Metamor-
phoses* of Ovid was a more profitable venture than was his brother
Edwin's earlier incursion into the publishing field, in which he
had no such protection. With a Letter Patent at his belt, he could
have spiked the piratical guns of William Stansby. Apparently
George Sandys profited by his brother's experience, and was not
daunted by it. But the whole question wants further consideration. One may question whether in such cases the author
generally undertook the sale and distribution of the book, or
whether the Letter Patent was not usually in effect a protection of
copy against piracy, enabling the author to deal more firmly with
the trade. Timothy Bright, for example, made John Windet,
the printer, his assign, and this seems to have been the normal
procedure. There was, again, the further complication of publishing by subscription, after the fashion of John Taylor the
Water-Poet.

III. HALLAM   AND   COLERIDGE   ON   THE   POST-
    HUMOUS BOOKS

   I append the following quotations for convenience of reference.
It is interesting to observe how the suspicions and suggestions in
one direction of Hallam and Coleridge compare with the conclusions to which I have been led in this study, though their
conception of 'the Church' is so far simplified as to prevent them
from envisaging opposition to Hooker's moderation in other
directions. Yet this appears to have been the determining factor
in the earlier history of the last three Books. Nor can I accept
Hallam's contemptuous references to Walton here and elsewhere
(in his *Introduction to the Literature of Europe*) as one 'credulous of
mere anecdote', for Walton took great pains to seek authenticity
in the material he used, and had a conscience in the matter. One
is grateful to Hallam for the monumental tribute which described
Hooker as 'one who mingled in these vulgar controversies like
a knight of romance among caitiff brawlers', but one is uneasy at
the thought that he could look upon the huge and vast significance
of the debate with averted, contemptuous eyes. It was not thus
that Hooker himself conceived of his life's work or, for that
matter, of either his allies or his opponents.

(i) HALLAM

These notions respecting the basis of political society, so far unlike what prevailed among the next generation of churchmen, are chiefly developed and dwelt upon in Hooker's concluding book, the eighth; and gave rise to rumour, very sedulously propagated soon after the time of its publication, and still sometimes repeated, that the posthumous portion of his work had been interpolated or altered by the puritans. For this surmise, however, I am persuaded that there is no foundation. The three latter books are doubtless imperfect, and it is possible that verbal changes may have been made by their transcribers or editors; but the testimony that has been brought forward to throw a doubt over their authenticity consists in those vague and self-contradictory stories which gossiping compilers of literary anecdote can easily accumulate.

The Constitutional History of England (1876), Vol. 1, pp. 220-21 (first printed in 1827).

If it be true, as it is alleged, that different manuscripts of the last three books did not agree, if even these disagreements were the result of fraud, why should he conclude that they were corrupted by the puritans rather than the church?...There is no reason to believe any other verbal changes to have been made in the loose draught which the author left...whatever changes were made, it does not appear that the manuscript was ever in the hands of the puritans.

Ib. p. 221, Note *d.*

I cannot but suspect that his whig principles in the last book are announced with a temerity that would have startled his superiors; and that its authenticity, however called in question, has been better preserved by the circumstances of its publication than if he had lived to give it to the world. Whitgift would probably have induced him to suppress a few passages incompatible with the servile theories already in vogue. It is far more usual that an author's genuine sentiments are perverted by means of his friends and patrons than of his adversaries.

Ib. p. 223.

(ii) COLERIDGE

It is a strange blind story this of the last three books, and of Hooker's live relict, the Beast without Beauty. But Saravia?—If honest Isaac's account of the tender, confidential, even confessional, friendship of Hooker and Saravia be accurate, how chanced it that Hooker did not entrust the manuscripts to his friend who stood beside him in his last moments? At all events, Saravia must have known whether they had or had not received the author's last hand. Why were not Mr Charke and the other

Canterbury parson called to account, or questioned at least as to the truth of Mrs Joan's story? Verily, I cannot help suspecting that the doubt cast on the authenticity of the latter books by the high church party originated in their dislike of portions of the contents.—In short, it is a blind story, a true Canterbury tale, dear Isaac!

The Literary Remains of Samuel Taylor Coleridge, ed. by H. N. Coleridge (London, 1838), Vol. III, pp. 19–20 (note upon Keble's 1836 edition of the *Polity* and of Walton's *Life*).

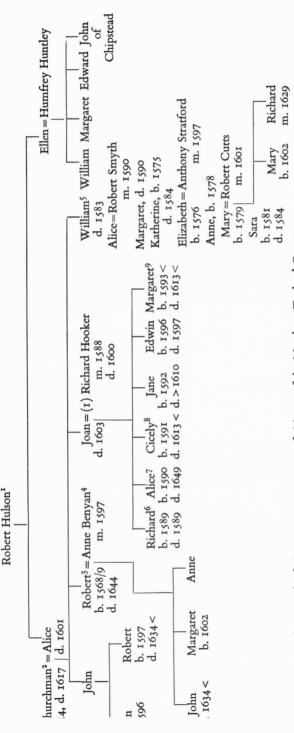

Pedigree I. CHURCHMAN—HOOKER

Robert Hulson[1]

Ellen = Humfrey Huntley

...hurchman[2] = Alice
...4, d. 1617 | d. 1601

William Margaret Edward John
of Chipstead

William[5] William Margaret Edward John
d. 1583

Alice = Robert Smyth
m. 1590

Margaret, d. 1590
Katherine, b. 1575
d. 1584

Elizabeth = Anthony Stratford
b. 1576   m. 1597

Anne, b. 1578

Mary = Robert Cutts
b. 1579   m. 1601

Sara
b. 1581
d. 1584

Mary   Richard
b. 1602   m. 1629

John

Robert
b. 1597
d. 1634 <

Robert[3] = Anne Benyan[4]
b. 1568/9   m. 1597
d. 1644

Joan = (1) Richard Hooker
d. 1603   m. 1588
              d. 1600

Richard[6] Alice[7]   Cicely[8]   Jane   Edwin   Margaret[9]
b. 1589   b. 1590   b. 1591   b. 1592   b. 1596   b. 1593 <
d. 1589   d. 1590   d. 1613 < d. >1610 d. 1597   d. 1613 <
                      d. 1649

...n
.596

John   Margaret
. 1634 <   b. 1602

Anne

[2] Master of the Merchant Taylors' Company, 1569.
...ster of the Merchant Taylors' Company, 1594.
...adle of the Merchant Taylors' Company, 1617–44.
[4] Daughter of Richard Benyan, Merchant Taylor.
...prized on 19 February 1589, according to the Register of St Andrew's: buried on '2' February 1589, according to the Register of St Andrew's, Enfield. The '2' is probably an entry lacking the second digit, e.g. '25', '25' or '28'.
...ed unmarried, but said by Huntley to have been betrothed to Thomas Langley in 1618.
...id to have married a Mr Chaloner, but with no confirmation.
...id by Walton to have married Ezechiel Chark, Vicar of Harbledown: other accounts name William Chark, Fellow of Peterhouse.
...Described as 'Elizabeth' in one set of documents, probably by confusion with Mrs Elizabeth Stratford.

[5] At Corpus Christi in 1581.

Pedigree II. SANDYS—EVELEIGH—EVINGTON

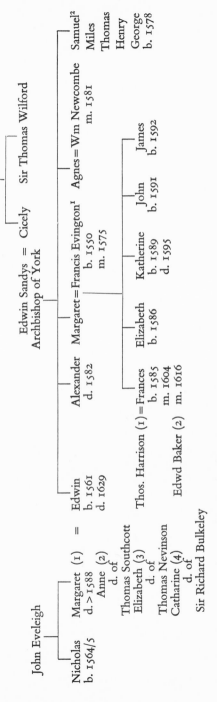

Notes. [1] Master of the Merchant Taylors' Company in 1609.
[2] The probable order of the birth of the Archbishop's family was: Samuel, Margaret, Agnes, Edwin, ending with George.

Pedigree III. NETHERSOLE

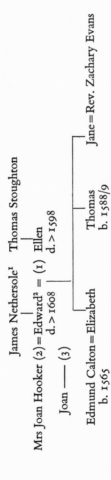

James Nethersole[1]   Thomas Stoughton

Mrs Joan Hooker (2) = Edward[2] = (1) Ellen
                          d. > 1608   d. > 1598

Joan —— (3)

Edmund Calton = Elizabeth   Thomas   Jane = Rev. Zachary Evans
          b. 1565   b. 1588/9

Notes.   [1] Mayor of Canterbury in 1572 and 1579.   [2] Mayor of Canterbury in 1590 and 1604.

Index